An Introduction to
AL-ISLAM
and
ISLAMIC LAW

by Dr. Muhamad Mugraby

Copyright © 2013 Muhamad Mugraby
First Edition 2013
All Rights Reserved.

ISBN: 0615696783
ISBN-13: 9780615696782

Published by the author in Charleston, South Carolina,
United States of America, and available from Amazon.com,
Createspace.com and many retailers.

Printed in the United States of America

TABLE OF CONTENTS

Foreword . . . . *vii*
Introduction . . . . *xvii*

Section One
Al-Islam 1
  Al-Islam, a General View *3*
  Bearing Witness to Allah *15*
  At-tanzeel: Al-Quran, Ar-Resalat *27*

Section Two
Selections from Al-Quran Interpreted 37
  Surat Al-Fatiha *39*
  Surat Al-Alaq *61*
  Ayat Al-Kursi *67*

Section Three
Creed: Meaning Belief and Charity 71
  The Meaning of Creed *73*
  Creed: Meaning Belief *79*
  The Good Names of Allah *83*

Section Four
Creed: Meaning Al-Haqq and Al-Sharia 93
Al-Haqq *95*
The Hukm of Allah *101*
The Original Al-Qawa-ed Al-Kulliat
  of Al-Sharia *109*
Rule Development under Al-Qawa-ed Al-Kulliat
  of Al-Sharia: Role of Al-Fiqh *139*
Accountability: The Promise, the Warning, and the
  Recompensation *143*
Clemency: Al-Safh through Al-Afou, Al-Ghifran and
  Al-Tawbat *147*

Section Five
Creed: Meaning the Nation and the State 151
Al-Ummat *153*
The Islamic State *157*

Section Six
The Relationship of Muslims and Non-Muslims in Dar Al-Islam 173
The Relationship with Apostates *175*
The Relationship with Ahl-ul-zimmat *177*
The Relationship with Al-Kuffar *183*
The Rule of Al-Sharia Suspended In Lebanon:
  a Case Study *185*

Section Seven
The Relationship of Muslims and Non-Muslims Out of Dar Al-Islam 203
Dar Al-Ahd and Dar Al-Harb *205*
Muslims out of Dar Al-Islam *209*

*Should There Be One Muslim State in
    Dar Al-Islam?* *211*

Section Eight
Al-Islam and Human Rights **213**
    A Brief History of Human Rights in the West . . *215*
    *A Discussion of the Western Approach to Human
      Rights and Al-Islam* *217*
    The State of Human Rights in the West *221*
    *A Comparison between Human Rights in the West
      and Al-Qawa-ed Al-Kulliat of Al-Sharia* . . *227*
    The Issue of Re-compensation for Theft. *231*

About the Author **235**

Index **237**

FOREWORD

I have been driven to author this book by many motivations.

I am a Muslim. I am also a human rights advocate and defender. I am a jurist.

As a Muslim, I have found from experience that many Muslims are not educated enough about Al-Islam.

More particularly, some Muslims who are of the younger generations have been mainly influenced by Western cultures, as they were educated in Western schools which provided them with little or no education about Al-Islam.

As to non-Muslims, Al-Islam has been inaccurately and unfairly pictured as something very different from what it truly is. This unfortunate fact has negatively influenced many in the West, including some Muslims, and poisoned their minds with respect to Al-Islam.

Thus, a thick cloud of ignorance and misrepresentation has, for no rational reason, served the double purpose of alienating many Muslims from Al-Islam and of giving rise to animosity against Al-Islam by some non-Muslims. I do not intend to absolve many Muslims who, knowingly or by default, participated in this campaign either maliciously or through their own faulty interpretations and misrepresentation of Al-Islam. As a result of all the foregoing, conflicts between Muslims and non-Muslims were started or fueled. Many of those conflicts were of a bloody nature. I find these results outrageous, particularly as they unfortunately continue to recur without an end in sight.

As a human rights advocate and jurist, I have come to increasingly appreciate that Al-Islam is vastly ahead of the Universal Declaration of Human Rights of 1948 and the French Declaration of the Rights of Man and the Citizen of 1887, and that many more such rights are safeguarded by Al-Sharia than in those two declarations, as well as in the European Convention on Human Rights of 1950.

I have come to increasingly realize that the tabling of the issue of human rights constitutes by itself significant progress by non-Muslims in the direction of Al-Islam. This progress has been slow but nevertheless ought to be welcomed.

This is in direct conflict with the prevailing "wisdom" in the West consisting of accusations and/or insinuations which have been frequently and freely promoted about the alleged general backwardness of Muslims and their lack of conformity with human rights. Many "orientalists" who knew little Arabic falsely proclaimed themselves to be experts on Al-Islam. They criticized Al-Islam on unscientific grounds, but their criticisms were mostly delivered to their Western audiences and filtered from there to some "enlightened" Muslims. After the events of 9/11, the circle of criticism widened immensely as a new breed of self-styled orientalists joined the fray and promoted the ideology that Al-Islam fosters an aggressive mission that threatens Western nations and Western civilization.

Some of the old as well as the new groups of Western critics of Al-Islam succeeded in coining, and spreading through their writings and/or the media new terminology, adopted first by the Western collective consciousness, and subsequently by many "enlightened" Arabs and Muslims. This terminology has the effect of encouraging a culture of Islamophobia. A sample of these terms is: *Islamist, jihadist,* and *fundamentalist.* All of these are allegedly natural leaders of actual or potential terrorists or potential recruits for the same. Terrorism became the lead heading of most of the published "studies" that embody a great deal of the modern Western criticism of Al-Islam. It became so ridiculous that every Muslim became a potential or actual terrorism suspect. This is an outrage.

Even the term *madrassat,* which is Arabic for school, was demonized. This word is often applied to a small preschool class that is traditionally annexed to mosques and is frequented mostly by disadvantaged children. These innocent, basic educational entities were dubbed bedrocks of terrorism!

In geography, the term "Near East" was coined first, followed by the term "Middle East." Both terms were intended to replace the classical term *Mashreq* and historic term *Bilad-ush-Sham.* "North Africa" replaced the *Great Maghreb.* All these terms were then merged in a new one: "MENA," which stands for Middle East and North Africa, replacing the term "Arab World." Many other terms were and continue to be developed and taken up by many Arabs and Muslims who unwittingly participated and continue to participate in making them standard.

All such efforts serve to enhance, both ignorantly and/or intentionally, the drive to separate Muslims from their original culture and increasingly alienate them from Al-Islam. This prophecy is to be found in the *Ayat*:

> Many of the People of the Book, who developed personal envy after they realized the truth of the message, would like to cause you to defect from your belief and become infidel. Do pardon and forgive them until Allah makes His decision. (*Al-Baqarat* 109)

What we are witnessing is a modern campaign with ancient roots. It started in the nineteenth century with the French Napoleonic invasion of Egypt and Syria and was followed by the century-long French occupation of Algeria and the attempt to wrestle it away from Al-Islam. In parallel, Western institutions of secondary and higher education were established in many Arab and Muslim countries under Western management and financing. They were mostly organized and led by Christian missionaries from North America and Europe. The French model in Algeria was followed by the Ataturk model in Turkey, the Pahlavi model in Iran, and many hybrid models in other countries, including Egypt and Lebanon.

One of the strategies of this campaign targets the Arabic language and has the object of eliminating it. This happened in Algeria, Tunisia, Morocco, and Turkey. In other countries the alternative was to greatly diminish its influence. This happened in Lebanon and the Gulf and to a large extent in Egypt. The reason for targeting Arabic is that it is the original language of Al-Quran and hence of Al-Islam and the basic medium for preserving the indigenous culture of Muslims. An Arab who does not understand Arabic will not understand Al-Quran.

It is not overreaching to conclude that the ultimate object of this campaign is to alter the loyalty of Muslims, consciously or unconsciously, but mostly unconsciously, by transferring it away from Al-Islam and into the West, led by the United States of America. In the best possible scenario, this campaign has the effect of corrupting the loyalty of Muslims and making it a hybrid. Unfortunately, those whose loyalty is so altered or otherwise corrupted get nothing from the West in return. It is such a poor trade. The best it can yield is to reinforce Muslim subservience to the West under one name or another.

One of the great strengths of Al-Islam is its strong pluralistic nature. This great historic quality is mostly ignored in the West. It is significantly disregarded that Al-Islam recognizes earlier religions such as Judaism and Christianity and esteems their prophets, such as Jesus, David, and Moses, as messengers and prophets of Al-Islam, too. Such recognition is of the essence of belief under Al-Islam. This is what, in practical terms, protected Christianity in Muslim lands, with all its churches, institutions, and parishes, and continues to protect the freedom of Christians of all denominations to practice their religion in those lands. In fact, all Christian churches that exist today on Muslim lands were built under Islamic governance. Unfortunately, Christian churches do not reciprocate by recognizing Muhammad as the Prophet and Messenger of Allah that he is.

Moreover, mosques in Western countries where there is a Christian majority are subject to restrictions that do not apply to churches in Muslim lands. For example, some Western governments ban the construction of minarets as part of the mosques. Many ban the *azan*, while church bells in Muslim lands ring without restriction side by side with the *azan* from the minarets of mosques.

One of the worst things that happened to the Arabic language is the corruption of meaning in the translation of terms from and to other languages. In the process, much of the basic Arabic vocabulary was abused. Some meanings were totally reversed.

The most significant example is the name Allah, which is equally used by all religions in the region, and the word Al-Sharia, which is Arabic for "law" or "legislation." The various derivatives of *Al-Sharia* are still used as basic legal terms in Arab and Islamic countries. The Islamic tradition highly valued Al-Sharia as a pillar of human society.

Al-Sharia is chiefly concerned with protecting the sanctity of life, the sanctity of private property, and the sanctity of contracts. Under the heading of contract, one does not only find private contracts and promises but also constitutional contracts and international treaties. The most famous constitutional contract in Islamic history is the pact that was entered into by the Prophet Muhammad and the three groups that constituted the population of Al-Madina: the Muslim immigrants from Mecca, the Muslims of Al-Madina, and the Jewish tribes of Al-Madina. It stated that together, the three groups constituted an independent nation, and it set forth the rights and obligations of the citizens and groups thereunder. The major towns that were taken by the Muslims as part of what is known as the *Futouh,* the plural of the Arabic word *Fat-h* that means the "opening up" but is commonly and erroneously translated as "conquest," were opened to the Muslims peacefully under written pacts with the community elders of each town, where the Muslims pledged to protect the security of their lives and property. Hence the early, spectacular Islamic *Futouh* were never accompanied by bloodshed among civilians or the destruction of cities. Thus Al-Sharia maintained and greatly expanded upon the earlier culture of the covenants that distinguished the traditions of the prophets Ibrahim and Moses. But unlike those covenants, the Islamic contracts were made with and among people and not between prophets and God.

Another example of abuse in translation is to be found in the words *da-en* and *madeen*, which became legal terms. In Arabic, *da-en* means the obligor of the debt, the debtor, and *madeen* the owner of the debt, the creditor. But in the newest legal terminology translated from French and under French influence, each term took the meaning of the other!

From the dawn of Islamic era following the *Futouh*, a legal regime was put in place to protect the non-Muslim minorities, called *ahd-ul-zimmat*. Church and temple leaderships enjoyed great autonomy in their respective religious communal matters and original jurisdiction over family law, and cooperated closely with the Islamic state's political leadership. Most of the Christian churches of the Middle East had and continue to have deep roots in the Islamic world.

Finally and naturally, I do not consider myself, as a Muslim, a savage or a terrorist. By the same token, I do not consider my fellow Muslims backward people, savages, or terrorists. I disagree with all the names they have been called which belittle their relationship to Al-Islam or slander the persons who are called by these names.

Furthermore, I strongly disagree with the pushing of Muslims away from their roots, culture, and identity by pushing them away from Al-Islam.

Dr. Muhamad Mugraby

Hence I have determined that there is an urgent need to cast a new light on the message of Al-Islam in order to support the right of all Muslims to full loyalty to Al-Islam and to the preservation and protection of their Islamic identity, through safeguarding or regaining their Islamic conscience and human dignity as Muslims and bringing down the walls of separation between Muslims and Al-Islam which were built or are being pursued by elements that are openly unsympathetic or hostile to Al-Islam.

I address all Muslims in all their lands or in the lands of others. Muslims have to realize fully that it is both their right and duty to be Muslim, that the message they belong to is great, and that they have every right to take credit for following it. But they also need to learn more about it.

I equally address the non-Muslims who know little or have been misled about Al-Islam. It is also their right and duty to learn about true Al-Islam. This would be of great benefit to them and to all humanity. They should not expect, as they may have been wrongly led to believe, any evil from Al-Islam or from true Muslims.

I especially wish to address the new generations of Muslims, and more particularly those who graduated from American and European schools and universities like my wife, my children, and I did.

I hope and pray that this humble contribution of mine will help put us all on the right path.

Beirut, 15 Ramadan 1432 H.   Muhamad Mugraby

INTRODUCTION

There are simply countless works on the subject of Al-Islam, old and contemporary. A large part of these works remains in the form of manuscripts yet to be reviewed and/or printed. This book is not intended to make a presentation that questions or supersedes preexisting treatises. Furthermore, it is not a university dissertation constantly requiring a discussion of earlier works and carefully providing references.

The purpose of this book is to complement the existing books on Al-Islam by highlighting certain of its aspects, perhaps from other angles. It is hoped that this will fill some of the void in the appreciation by many earlier authors of Al-Islam as presented in the message that the Prophet Muhammad launched in his capacity as Messenger of Allah to all His creation. My point of departure in this voyage is the original source, the revelation called Al-Quran. It is the principal source of Al-Sharia and *hukmul-lah*, the rule of Allah, and my principal guide. Al-Sharia gave us the original *al-qawa-ed al-kulliat*, which do not change, are inalienable, and remain valid for all times and places. In modern terms it is above constitutions and statutes because it is their original and supreme source.

The more detailed *qawa-ed* and rules are the product of the *fuqaha'*, plural of *faqih*, especially by those who founded schools of *fiqh* for the purpose of upholding the original *al-qawa-ed al-kulliat*. Much of *fiqh* also took its legitimacy from the sayings and conduct of Prophet Muhammad, known as *Al-Hadith* or *Sunnat-ul-Rasoul* or simply *Sunnat*, as an authority held by the preponderance of *fiqh* to be equally authoritative to Al-Quran. It is validly assumed, however, that the Prophet could not contradict the revelation but was able to complement it. What is not evidenced by Al-Quran or *Sunnat* is definitely related to certain factors of time, place, and socioeconomic conditions, and hence capable of change. The role of the *fuqaha'* puts them on par with legislators in the modern sense.

It should be conceded that there is some difficulty in interpreting the language of Al-Quran for Arabic-speaking Muslims and much difficulty in translating it to other languages. The task of interpretation and translation should not be confined to providing the individual with the apparent linguistic meaning of words and phrases, but such linguistic meaning should be used as the springboard for realizing its basic meaning and its cause-and-effect relationship with *al-qawa-ed al-kulliat* of Al-Sharia.

Dr. Muhamad Mugraby

Al-Quran was revealed in classical Arabic prose, which constitutes the standard measure of the Arabic language as well as the measure of excellence of all Arabic prose for all times. Someone who has not read Al-Quran cannot be very fluent in Arabic. Moreover, the various interpretations of Al-Quran that we have are written mostly in an old style which is often hard to comprehend. The translations into other languages have mostly used old styles which are plagued with errors due to the often poor comprehension of Quranic Arabic and the difficulty in finding the right equivalent of the Arabic words and phrases in the language to which the translation is made. In fact, many of those words and phrases simply have no exact or even close equivalent in other languages. The errors are compounded by later translators' copying from earlier translators.

What I have opted for is to have before me, side by side with Al-Quran, copies of leading classical Arabic lexicons such as *Lisan Al-Arab*, *Muheet-ul-Muheet*, and *Taj Al-Arous*. I found *Lisan Al-Arab* to be the most helpful.

Going through these great reference books reveals not only the multiplicity of meanings which is characteristic of Arabic and which might tend to confuse, but also the wide range of complementary meanings contributed by derivatives of the same root. In the end Arabic is more logical, mathematical, and architectural than most languages, yet it is flowery and artistically beautiful. It conveys its meanings in a way unlike any other language, a way difficult for non-natives to master. This is why

I have generally insisted on using original Arabic terms, transliterated, and refrained from depending on equivalents borrowed from the English language. Each word has a depth and breadth of its own tied to particular sets of roots and background from its own cultural foundations and springs of knowledge. What I attempted to do was to give each such Arabic word the best explanatory translation I could find in the English language. Therefore, this book is loaded with Arabic terms in Latin characters.

It is easy to come to the conclusion that Al-Quran is not only a book of prayers, basic religious beliefs, and Al-Sharia, but also an extensive summation in the modern legal sense embodying general principles, reasoning, pleadings, logic, and evidence in support of the contents of the message of Al-Islam so that believing in Al-Islam is based on reason and rational conclusions and not steered largely by dogma. All this is made in an encyclopedic setting combining rich literary prose with tales, precedents, examples, and comparisons which constitute a very delicate and beautiful product. In this context, Al-Sharia is spelled out very clearly, easily penetrating the hearts and minds of the readers or listeners. This is much more compelling and attractive than using the dull style of "article one." "article two," and so on that is typical of European codes and statutes that were used as the models from which modern laws of the Arab and Islamic worlds were copied.

There is no question that Al-Quran is very influential over the political and social consciousness of

Dr. Muhamad Mugraby

Muslims and is the pillar of Muslim culture. Muslims learn from it the commandments of Allah, including the basics of the religion and Al-Sharia. In less advantaged Muslim countries, the simple Quranic schools attached to mosques continue to teach reading, writing, and the worship of Allah. This enabled Algeria to withstand 132 years of French colonialism which was bent on changing the natural and original identity of the country. The *Mujahideen* who fought the French until liberation in 1962 consisted mostly of attendees of those schools and not of French schools. Near the end of that year I had the opportunity and privilege to witness the raising of the Algerian flag over the UN headquarters in New York City, where I was a graduate student of law.

I am not concerned in this book with tracing the detailed history of the application of Al-Sharia, nor with the degree to which it was actually observed or not observed by the various sultans and princes. The conduct of sultans and princes is something for which they are to be held personally accountable and does not change their duty to uphold and obey Al-Sharia, which is the source of their legitimacy and which they cannot change

There is no doubt that the culture of Al-Islam decisively influenced and enriched human civilization within and outside Dar Al-Islam. It was not exclusive to Muslims. It also witnessed the active participation in this civilization of non-Muslims who lived in peace and harmony in hospitable Muslim lands and enjoyed all the safeguards to which Muslims are entitled under Al-Sharia, beginning with the freedom of religion.

This book also will not be particularly concerned with the affairs or rituals of worship such as prayers, fasting, and pilgrimage because these are quite standard and clear. Nevertheless, it should be pointed out that *Al-Hajj* is a unique annual convention for Muslims who gather together from all corners of the earth, and each year it boasts millions of participants. "They come from every remote road dug deep in between mountains" (*Al-Hajj* 27). Such a convention is a pure act of worship. It could also include cultural seminars to bring about the exchange of ideas and knowledge that unquestionably was originally meant to be part of *Al-Hajj*.

The best way to conclude this introduction is to quote from Muhammad Asad, the Austrian Jew who became a Muslim and spent most of his time in Muslim lands, ending with distinguished service in Pakistan's diplomatic corps. This quotation expresses a conviction that I share with him.

> Islam appears to me like a perfect work of architecture. All its parts are harmoniously conceived to complement and support each other; nothing is superfluous and nothing is lacking; and the result is a structure of absolute balance and solid composure.

Section One

AL-ISLAM

Chapter One

AL-ISLAM, A GENERAL VIEW

A name often describes in summary the nature and object of the thing. Hence it is best to commence with a description of the linguistic meaning in Arabic of the word Al-Islam.

The root of the word is the verb *salama*. Its various nouns mean peace, such as in *as-salam*, and security, such as in *as-salamat*. *As-salam* also means innocence and ingenuousness. *As-salam* applies to individuals as well as to groups or nations. It is the opposite of harm and violence. It is Allah's peace on earth.

> "All you believers: join the peace without exception." (*Al-Baqarat* 208)

Security is meant for the individual as well as for groups. Both terms, peace and security, are the opposite of conflict, war, and violence and ensure the liberty of the individual and the group. Security starts with innocence as well as with mental and physical integrity. Innocence means the lack of harm and evil. *As-salam*, the peace, is one of the Good Names of Allah.

> "Allah is the sole divinity, the Holy Potentate, the Peace, and the Empowerer." (*Al-Hashr* 23)

Furthermore, *as-salamat* means the state of being wholesome, free of defects.

> "Allah calls to the house of peace." (*Younus* 25)

That is where everyone is secure and free from fear.

As-salam does not only manifest itself outwardly but also internally in the state of security, *salamat*, of the heart and the state of innocence, *bara-at*, from evil ideas and intentions.

> "Except whoever comes to Allah with an innocent heart..." (*Ash-shuara'* 89)

The word "innocent" is a translation from the Arabic adjective *saleem*, the attribute of the noun *salamat*. *As-salam* is the state of safety, integrity, and the lack of fault. The house of *as-salam*, as in *Younus* 25, is nothing but paradise.

At-tasleem is derived from *as-salam*. It takes place by verbally directing *as-salam* to a person. The least of its multiple meanings is offering an assurance of peace in the form of the standard greeting: *as-salamu alaykum*, which means "peace be with you for I bring you no harm." This is the most widely used form of greeting in the Arab and Islamic worlds. A *tasleem* may also be directed at a prophet, using the third person: *alayhee as-salam*, which means "may he be in peace." The most prominent meaning of *tasleem* is professing one's obedience to Al-Sharia and commitment to the *Ar-resalat* carried by the Prophet Muhammad the Messenger of Allah. There is a necessary and logical relationship between those two confessions. Someone who believes in Allah and professes full obedience to Him must also be committed to the descendent *Ar-resalat*, the *Tanzeel*, and amplified by the conduct of the Prophet, his *Sunnat*. In short, he submits to Al-Sharia.

Al-musa-lamat, another derivative of *Salam*, is "making peace." *As-Salam*, "the peace," means the absence, or end, of conflict. *Al-Islam* is the act of joining the peace by confessing acceptance of *Ar-Resalat* or submitting in peace to Allah:

> "All you believers: join the peace without exception." (*Al-Baqarat* 208)
>
> "Enter [Paradise] with peace and security." (*Al-Hijr* 46)
>
> "What is a better creed to have than to submit oneself in peace to Allah?" (*An-Nisa'* 125)

> "He said I have submitted in peace to Rab-il-Alameen." (*Al-Baqarat* 131)

Becoming a Muslim means attaining a state of peace with oneself, peace with humanity, peace with the Prophet, and peace with Allah under one uniting banner, which is Al-Islam.

Yet there could be a difference between Al-Islam and belief.

> "The Bedouins said: We have believed. Say: You have not believed. You have only joined the peace but belief is yet to enter your hearts." (*Al-Hujurat* 14)

Whoever professes adherence to Al-Sharia is, on the face of it, a Muslim. Belief, however, is true faith. It is in the heart. He who has it is called a believer. One may possibly be a Muslim in appearance but not a true believer in his heart. What really matters is belief. The Arabic word for belief is *al-eeman*, which is derived from *al-amanat*, which in turn means honesty or confidence. One who believes in his heart what he expresses in his mouth or behavior shall have demonstrated his *eeman*. If not, he bears the guilt of deceit which is for Allah alone to judge. It is said: Al-Islam is in the tongue, but belief is in the heart.

The Prophet Muhammad was not the only prophet who was entrusted with the message of Al-Islam, but he was the last of the prophets. It is said that all prophets were entrusted with Al-Islam but their respective *shara-i'*, plural of *sharia*, differed. Each of them sat in judgment according to his book:

> "The Prophets who submitted to the peace judge by it." (*Al-Maidat* 44)

Ibrahim was the first of the Muslims:

> "I am the first of the Muslims." (*Al-Anaam* 163)

> "Ibrahim was not a Jew or a Christian. He was not a polytheist. He was a Muslim *hanif.*" (*Al-Omran* 67)

A *hanif* is someone who is inclined to be righteous. He takes the side of right without hesitation. He is straightforward. The meaning of the above *Ayat* is that the Prophet Ibrahim became drawn to the faith of Allah, Al-Islam. Thus a *hanif* is the Muslim who is steadfast in his adherence to Al-Islam. The *hanif* creed is nothing but Al-Islam.

In other words, Al-Islam is the acceptance of, and the professing of obedience to, the highest authority in the universe, that is Allah, who has no associate in His authority. Allah's authority is the source of Al-Sharia and the basis of its legitimacy. Any allegation of multiple authorities constitutes polytheism, *shurk*, which challenges the core belief of Al-Islam based on the unity of Allah and His lack of family or associates. Al-Quran makes the case that had there been more than one divine authority in the universe, it would have led to conflict, contradiction, and warring among such alleged authorities.

> "Allah did not adopt a child, and there is no other divinity with him. Otherwise each divinity would have taken off with what it created, and they would have formed a hierarchy." (*Al-Mou'minoon* 91)

> "Had there been [on Earth and in Heavens] divinities apart from Allah they [Earth and Heavens] would have been corrupted." (*Al-Anbia'* 22)

Thus the unity of Allah and the singularity of His authority are the guaranty of equality and peace among human beings and the integrity of the universal system as a whole under the care and protection of Allah.

Al-Islam is the creed of equality among humans, men and women. They congregate in equality for prayer behind the *imam*, which means "the leader." They perform the *Hajj*, which means the pilgrimage to Mecca, without discrimination. More importantly, Muslims are equal before Al-Sharia. Al-Sharia applies to them equally. There is no discrimination between the white and the nonwhite, the poor and the rich, the noble and the commoner, and the male and the female.

The *Ayat*—"Men are *qawamoon* upon women" (*An-Nisa'* 34)—has often been interpreted as giving men authority over their women. I have translated the Arabic *qawamoon* to mean "shall sustain and take full care of women and treat them justly." It is part of men's obligation as heads of their respective family units to provide for and protect their family members with emphasis on the women, who are the mothers, wives, daughters, and sisters.

Al-Islam is a universal creed, with a view to the entire universe:

> "To Allah belong the East and the West. You face him wherever you turn. Allah is so boundless and so all-knowing." (Al-Baqarat 115)

As one of the goals of al-Islam is the establishment of comprehensive peace, *Salam*, among all individuals and groups, one must accept the idea that *tableegh*, which means giving notice and spreading the word, of Al-Islam in the universe is an Islamic duty. We must then define what constitutes the state of peace under Al-Islam.

The state of peace is diametrically opposed to the state of oppression, *zulm*. The original meaning of the verb *zalama*, a derivative of *zulm*, is to replace the shining light of the day, *an-noor*, by the darkness of night, *az-zalam*. *Zulm* violates Al-Sharia because it results from taking the path of desires and overpowering right such as by misplacing things in time, place, quantity, or quality; by deceit; or by otherwise deviating from the right path. It is equivalent to the obstruction, frustration, or outward usurpation of right. Peace and oppression cannot coexist.

Thus, establishing the state of peace mandates prevention of oppression and doing away with oppressors. It is like taking human beings out of darkness, *az-zalam*, and into the shining light, *an-noor*.

> "With His leave, He takes them out of the depth of darkness and into the shining light and guides them unto the straight path." (*Al-Maidat* 16)

> "Allah is the shining light of Heavens and Earth." (*An-Noor* 35)

> "Allah is the guardian of the believers. He takes them out of the depth of darkness and unto the shining light." (*Al-Baqarat* 257)

Committing aggression toward others in fulfillment of the oppressor's desires is an act of *zulm*.

> "The oppressors pursued their desires." (*Ar-Room* 29)

Many human beings tend to be oppressive if they are convinced that they have the power to violate with impunity the rights of others who can offer no resistance, or that they will get away with it.

"The Human is prone to oppression." (*Ibrahim* 34)

This is where Al-Sharia intervenes to repulse oppression and restore the state of peace.

> "The oppressive people were routed." (*Al-In' am* 45)
>
> "We will make the oppressors suffer." (*Al-Kahf* 87)
>
> "We punished the oppressors for their transgression with painful suffering." (*Al-A'raf* 165)
>
> "Woe to the oppressors! They shall be tormented on a painful day." (*Al-Zukhruf* 65)
>
> "The curse of Allah shall fall on the oppressors." (*Al-A'raf* 44)

Allah dislikes oppression and does not oppress:

> "Allah does not oppress even to the measure of a single atom." (*An-Nisa'* 40)
>
> "Allah does not oppress humans at all." (*Younus* 44)

"Allah wishes no oppression on His worshippers." (*Ghafer* 31)

Here are examples of oppression:

(1) Polytheism, *shurk*, i.e., that Allah has associates or that he is one of many divinities.

"Do not be a polytheist, for polytheism is great oppression." (*Luqman* 13)

Disregarding Al-Sharia.

"Those who do not judge by what Allah commanded are oppressors." (*Al-Ma'edat* 45)

(3) Driving believers out of their homes.

"Those who were unrightfully driven out of their homes…" (*Al-Hajj* 40)

(4) Committing a crime for which a punishment is prescribed.

"Those who violate the bounds set by Allah are the oppressors." (*Al-Baqarat* 229)

"He who inherits a victim of a killing has the authority [to demand recompensation]." (*Al-Isra'* 33)

(5) Concealment of testimony.

"He is most oppressive who conceals his testimony from Allah." (*Al-Baqarat* 140)

(6) Bearing witness is a primary and original Islamic duty. Allah addresses the Prophet Muhammad:

"We have sent you to be a witness." (*Al-Ahzab* 45)

Allah is the witness, *Shaheed*.

"Allah is sufficient witness." (*Al-Fateh* 28)

(7) Giving false testimony, such as in perjury. False speech in general is such a major offense to Al-Islam that it is considered comparable to disbelieving in the unity of Allah.

"Those who worship *Ar-Rahman* do not testify falsely..." (*Al-Firqan* 72)

"Avoid false speech." (*Al-Hajj* 30)

(8) Enticing evil, *al-baghyy*, such as by corruption or other immoral ways. A derivative of *baghyy* is *bigha'*, which means lewdness or prostitution.

"Those who oppress people and entice evil on Earth shall be painfully tormented." (*Al-Shura* 279)

(9) Doing usury.

"If you repent you will only recover your net capital asset so that you do not oppress and are not oppressed." (*Al-Baqarat* 279)

Chapter Two

BEARING WITNESS TO ALLAH

There is a consensus among Muslims that the first pillar of Al-Islam is "bearing witness, *Shahadat*, that there is no god but Allah, and that Muhammad is the Messenger, *rasool*, of Allah." This testimony, *Shahadat*, is mostly recited as part of the *azan*, which is a simple reminder of this pillar of Al-Islam and an imperative call, a summons, to prayer.

The *azan* consists of the testimony preceded twice by the phrase of *takbeer*: *Allahu Akbar*, another testimony which means "Allah is greater than everything," in fact *the* greatest. The compounding of the two testimonial phrases constitutes not only the pillar but also the founding stone of Al-Islam.

Testimony, *Shahadat*

Shahadat is derived from s*hahida*, which means acquired direct knowledge of something such as by seeing it, which is the literary meaning of the verb *shahida*. It is like seeing a star at night. A testimony has the necessary quality of honesty and credibility. Someone who bears witness knows consciously, understands, admits, affirms, and is obligated by his testimony.

When a Muslim bears witness that there is no divinity but Allah and that Muhammad is the Messenger of Allah, he enters into two solemn, earnest, obligating, and nonretractable covenants, the first with Allah and His Messenger, and the second with fellow Muslims.

> "You have affirmed and to this you shall testify." (*Al-Baqarat* 84)
>
> "They said we have affirmed. He said bear witness to that." (*Al Omran* 81)
>
> "We now believe in Allah and I bear witness that we are Muslim." (*Al Omran* 52)
>
> "Say: Bear witness that we are Muslim." (*Al Omran* 64)

Allah is a witness. One of His Good Names is *Shaheed*, which means "the ultimate witness." He makes His testimony in a way similar to that of humans.

> "Allah testified that there is no divinity but Allah." (*Al Omran* 18)

> "Allah testifies to what He sent down to you." (*An-Nisa'* 166)

> "Allah is the witness to everything." (*Al-Hajj* 17)

> "We are witnesses to everything you do." (*Younus* 61)

> "Allah is the witness to what they are doing." (*Younus* 46)

The Prophet Muhammad, Messenger of Allah, is a witness.

> "The Messenger shall be the witness testifying as to what you do." (Al-Baqarat 143)

> "We called you to be the witness as to those people." (*An-Nisa'* 41)

Individuals are witnesses as to each other.

> "We have made you a just *ummat* to be witnesses as to all individuals." (*Al-Baqarat* 143)

> "For the Messenger shall be a witness as to you and you shall be witnesses

> as to the [other] individuals." (*Al-Hajj* 87)

A witnessed day, *yaoum mash-hood*, is an eventful day when a large number of people are present and bear witness. It is also the Day of Judgment.

> "That will be the day for which all people shall be assembled. It is the day to be witnessed." (*Hood* 103)

A testimony is evidence to what individuals did and produces certain results under Al-Sharia as to both private and public rights and obligations.

> "Let the just among you testify." (*At-Talaq* 2)

> "Let there be witnesses when you buy from and sell to each other." (*Al-Baqarat* 282)

> "Four witnesses, at least, should be called to testify against the women." (*An-Nisa'* 15)

> "You shall call at least two of your men to bear witness." (*Al-Baqarat* 282)

> "Those who charge married women with adultery but are unable to bring four witnesses..." (*An-Noor* 4)

"Avoid false speaking." (*Al-Hajj* 30)

Thus, it is obligatory under Al-Sharia to bear witness truthfully.

Takbeer

Takbeer is the verbal statement of *Allahu Akbar*, another testimony that Allah is greater and more magnificent, which means "Allah is the greatest and most magnificent," *al-akbar*. In comparison, all things and beings, including rich people, military commanders, and kings, are exceptionally tiny. *Kibriya'* is the state of being *al-akbar*. Hence one of the Good Names of Allah is *Al-Mutakabber*, which is the quality of being *al-akbar*, "the most potent."

> "His, in Heavens and on Earth, is the dominion marked with overbearing dignity." (*Al-Jathiat* 37)

> "Say your Lord is greater." (*Al-Mudather* 3)

> "You shall appreciate the greatness of Allah from what He guided you to." (*Al-Baqarat* 185)

Allah is the most potent over Earth and the potentate of the entire universe.

> "Allah has the power over everything and to do all things." (*Al-Baqarat* 148)

> "Heavens and Earth and all that is between them belong to Allah." (*Al-Maedat* 17)

> "All that is in Heavens and on Earth belong to Allah." (*An-Nisa'* 126)

> "Allah has the upper say." (*At-Tawbat* 40)

> "Allah created everything and He is the guardian of everything." (*Al-Zumar* 72)

Istikbar and *takab-bur* describe the quality of falsely pretending to be *al-akbar*, and hence challenging the *kibriya'* of Allah by belittling the message of Al-Islam and Al-Sharia.

> "Those who belie and belittle our *Ayaat*..." (*Al-Araf* 36)

> "They pretended to be the greatest but they were culpable people." (*Al-Araf* 133)

> "They falsely pretended to be the greatest on Earth." (*Fusilat* 15)

> "You have been belittling His *Ayaat*." (*Al-An'am* 93)

One who displays *istikbar* is called *mustakber*. He is the opposite of *mustad'af*, a person deemed weak and inconsequential, and hence belittled by the *mustakber*.

One of the purposes of *takbeer* in every *azan*, that is call to prayer, is to remind every *mustakber* that he is tiny and inconsequential before Allah, and that Allah gives support to every *mustad'af* in resisting the *mustakber*.

> "The hand of Allah is above all their hands." (*Al-Fateh* 10)

There Is No Divinity but Allah

This testimony is a proclamation of the unity of Allah and the exclusivity of His high authority, *al-su'dud*, which may not be challenged or competed against. Had it not been for the said unity and exclusivity, the universe would have been corrupted and would have fallen apart.

> "Had there been divinities apart from Allah [on Earth and in Heavens] they [Earth and Heavens] would have been corrupted." (*Al-Anbia'* 22)

> "Allah holds Heavens and Earth lest they cease to exist." (*Fatir* 41)

> "Had *Al-Haqq* copied after their whims, Earth and Heavens would have been corrupted." (*Al-Mou'minoon* 71)

Al-Haqq is Allah. The unity of Allah is carefully highlighted throughout Al-Quran. The most famous and decisive expression of this unity appears in *Surat Al-Ikhlas*. Our best translation of *Al-Ikhlas* is "absolute devotion." It expresses very eloquently the first article of belief in Al-Islam: "Say Allah is one and the only one. Allah is eternal and He is the recourse. He did not bear children and He was not born. None was ever his equal."

Expressions of faith in Allah are to be found in many other Ayaat, such as:

> "Allah, who there is no divinity but Him, is the Giver and the Sustainer of life." (*Al-Baqarat* 255)

> "Your god is one and there is no divinity but Him: Ar-Rahman-ul-Raheem." (*Al-Baqarat* 163)

As the unity of Allah is the foundation of the universal system, it may not be denied, and *al-shurk*, polytheism, constitutes an unforgivable offense.

> "Worship Allah and do not associate anything with Him." (*An-Nisa'* 36)

> "Allah would not expunge the offense of *shurk*. He will expunge all lesser offenses of whoever He chooses. Committing *shurk* is a fabrication of extreme evil." (*An-Nisa* 48)

Muhammad Is the Messenger of Allah

The message brings knowledge characterized by calm reason and solid logic. It also brings directives and injunctions. Part of the knowledge is recognition of the Messenger, the Prophet Muhammad, and his mission and authority on behalf of Allah which was bestowed upon him by Allah. Hence Muhammad is not only the Messenger, but also part and parcel of the message of Allah. This, in summary, is the meaning of the testimony: Muhammad is the Messenger of Allah.

> "He sent His Messenger carrying guidance to the creed of *Al-Haqq*, and to distinguish it among all other creeds." (*At-Tawbat* 33)

> "We sent you to spread the good news and to give notice of *Al-Haqq*." (*Al-Baqarat* 119)

> "Oh Messenger give notice of what was sent down to you by your Lord." (*Al-Ma'edat* 67)

> "We do not send our messengers except as bearers of good news and to give notice." (*Al-An'am* 48)

> "Our messengers brought them the evidence." (*Al-Ma'edat* 32)

In several *Ayaat* the Prophet Muhammad is named the Messenger of Allah.

> "Muhammad the Messenger of Allah and his companions are stout against the dis-believers, but tender among each other." (*Al-Fateh* 29)

> "Muhammad is not the father of any of your men but the Messenger." (*Al-Ahzab* 40)

> "Muhammad is only the Messenger." (*Al Omran* 144)

> "Do believe in what was sent down to Muhammad. It is *Al-Haqq* from your Lord." (*Muhammad* 2)

> "Know all people: the Messenger has brought you *Al-Haqq* from your Lord." (*An-Nisa* 170)

Belief in Allah requires belief in the Prophet Muhammad and believing him.

> "Following the commands and guidance of the Messenger is obedience to Allah." (*An-Nisa* 80)

> "So that you believe in Allah and His Messenger…" (*Al-Fateh* 9)

Obedience to Allah requires obeying His Messenger and Prophet.

> "Allah will admit all who obey Him and His Messenger to Gardens with flowing rivers. Those who do not, He will punish them painfully." (*Al-Fateh* 17)

> "Say: Obey Allah and the Messenger." (*Al Omran* 32)

> "Obey Allah and obey the Messenger." (*Al-Ma'edat* 92)

The testimony that Muhammad is the Messenger of Allah is the basis of the legitimacy of the creed preached by the Messenger in the name of Allah *Ar-Rahman, Ar-Raheem* and endows him with the power and authority to relay the words of Allah to the entire universe, not on his own personal behalf but on behalf of Allah.

The purpose of the dispatch of messengers by Allah, including the Prophet Muhammad, was to lead humans to the straight path and teach them Al-Sharia so that when they violate it, they may not plead ignorance thereof.

> "The Messengers carried good news and gave notice so that people, after the coming of Messengers, could not plead before Allah [the

defense of ignorance of Al-Sharia]." (*An-Nisa* 165)

Al-Basmalat

Al-Basmalat is short for "in the name of Allah *Ar-Rahman, Ar-Raheem.*" It is the first *Ayat* of *Surat Al-Fatiha* and the opening phrase of every other *Surat* (with the exception of *Surat At-Tawbat*, which is deemed to be a continuation of *Surat Al-Anfal*). *Al-Basmalat* signifies that what follows it is authoritative, peaceful, and comforting to mankind.

> "The hearts of those who believe find comfort in the mention of Allah. Mentioning Allah brings tranquility to all hearts." (*Ar-Raad* 28)

In other words, what follows every *Basmalat* came from Allah, an assurance that the words that follow authentically represent the will of Allah and are blessed by Allah.

In Al-Quran, *Al-Basmalat* has another function, which is to serve as a sort of a bookmark between the various *Suwar*, plural of *Surat*. Furthermore, it distinguishes to the common people the *suwar* from the *Hadeeth*, the traditional sayings of the Prophet Muhammad.

Chapter Three

AT-TANZEEL: AL-QURAN, AR-RESALAT

Al-Quran is the book. The word comes from the imperative *iqra'*, which means "read!" This order has several objects which lead to the knowledge of the basics of *Ar-Resalat*, the message. Here are some of the meanings of *Iqra'*:

(1) Receive the message and pass it on.

(2) It is time! The root of *iqra'* is *qar'*, which means time. The Arabic word for the blowing of the wind is *aqrat ar-reeh*.

(3) Study, learn, and understand. It is said in Arabic, "Have you read poetry," which means, "Have you *studied* poetry?" Learning and understanding is *fiqh*.

(4) Devote yourself, *tanassak*, to the worship of Allah and observance of Al-Sharia.

(5) Gather and consolidate, which means to gather and consolidate humans to worship Allah and observe Al-Sharia. Al-Quran also got its name from consolidating all the *Suwar* and their content of Al-Sharia, other commandments, injunctions, and historic examples and precedents. Whatever is consolidated is to be read and recited. Together they constitute Al-Quran. "We are commanded to bring it together and to recite it" (*Al-Qyamat* 17).

Al-Quran consists of chapters, each of which is called *Surat*. Each *Surat* consists of subparts called *Ayat*. An *Ayat* is a complete piece of revelation received at any one time by the Prophet Muhammad.

As-Surat
A *Surat* is a derivative of the root *sawara*, of which *soor*, which means wall, is also derived. It consists of several *Ayaat* grouped together as in a walled chamber. *Surat* means the path or *Sunnat*, i.e., the *Sunnat* of Allah.

> "*Suratun* We sent down, commanded, and sent within it Ayaat in evidence."
> (*An-Noor* 1)

Al-Ayat

Ayat means literally a road sign posted alongside a road that leads to another *Ayat* to show travelers the correct path. In Al-Quran *Ayat* means evidence, lesson, example, and/or commandment.

> "To be *Ayat* for the believers and to guide you unto the straight path." (*Al-Fateh* 20)

It is from the root *ay*, which is an exclamation mark of the right answer to a question of what is reasonable or unreasonable, permitted or not permitted. *Ay* is also synonymous to "Oh!" when used to call someone. *Ay* of the sun is its light.

Furthermore, *Ay* is both used as an interrogatory and to denote the precise answer. Finally, *ay* is used to interpret the meaning of a preceding phrase by a following phrase. Another derivative of *ay* is the verb *awa*, which means to shelter. Its noun, *ma'wa*, means refuge. *Ayat* also means a miracle of Allah. *Ayaat* is the plural of *Ayat*.

> "That constitutes an *Ayat* for those who reason." (*Al-Nahl* 67)

> "We brought you an *Ayat* from your Lord." (*Taha* 47)

> "*Ayat* is evidence to those who reason." (*Al-'Ankaboot* 35)

> "Thus Allah manifests His *Ayaat* to people so that they abstain." (*Al-Baqarat* 187)

An *Ayat* may consist of one or more sentences. We often find one sentence split into two subsequent *Ayaat*.

At-tanzeel

The Quran is the *Tanzeel*, which means "that which was sent down from high up," i.e., from Allah.

> "We sent it down by the power of *Al-Haqq*, and it descended by that power." (*Al-Isra'* 105)

> "For Allah sent down the Book by the power of *Al-Haqq*." (*Al-Baqarat* 176)

> "He sent down to you, by the power of *Al-Haqq*, the Book that conforms to what He holds in His hands." (*Al Omran* 3)

> "The Book speaks by *Al-Haqq*." (*Al-Mou'minoon* 62)

> "We have sent you down the Book by the power of *Al-Haqq* to enable you to sit in judgment among people." (*An-Nisa'* 105)

Al-Kitab, Al-Fardd

Al-Kitab is the Book. The Book is Al-Quran. One who believes in Allah and His Messenger the Prophet Muhammad must also believe in *Al-Kitab*. The original meaning of Al-Kitab is "what is written," a one-sheet letter. It also means a compilation of several sheets in a book. It further means *Al-Fardd*, which means the commandment. Here are the most important meanings of *Al-Kitab*:

(1) The book of Allah sent down to the Prophet Muhammad, Al-Quran.
(2) One of the books sent down by Allah to the other prophets who preceded the Prophet Muhammad.
(3) The ledger of accounts of each human being that set forth the basis for the accounting for his deeds upon the Day of Judgment.
(4) Al-Sharia or any of its individual commandments preceded by the verb *kutiba*.

Here are examples from Al-Quran where the verb *kutiba* is used as an imperative, a commandment, or an injunction:

> "*Al-Qisas* for killings is commanded upon you." (*Al-Baqarat* 178)

> "Fasting is commanded upon you." (*Al-Baqarat* 183)

> "It is commanded upon you like it was commanded upon who lived before you." (*Al-Baqarat* 183)

> "It is commanded upon you that when one of you is near death to make a benevolent will to your parents and the closest relatives." (*Al-Baqarat* 180)

> "We have commanded them that a soul is for a soul." (*Al-Ma-edat* 45)

> "They said: Lord, why did you command us to do battle?" (*An-Nisa'* 77)

The book of every prophet contains Al-Sharia particular to him as sent down by Allah. This is why the followers of prophets who received such books are called People of the Book. Although Al-Sharia of Al-Islam is the final sharia and supersedes all earlier sharia, yet Al-Sharia of each earlier prophet remains binding on his own people, his *ummat*, unless they freely choose to abide by the Islamic Al-Sharia.

> "Every *ummat* is called to its Book." (*Al-Jathiat* 28)

> "Allah accepted the covenant of the prophets as to the Book I sent you." (*Al Omran* 81)

According to authoritative *Hadith*, Al-Sharia of each of the books of other prophets governs the relations among the particular people of the Book, which gives a wide measure of autonomy to each such People and supports their ongoing identity and right to worship according to their own practices. It should be noted that the prophets of the two most noted, but not the only, Peoples of the Book recognized by Al-Islam, Jews and Christians, are all prophets of Al-Islam as well.

What is most important is that *Al-Kitab* of *Allah* is what governs relations among individuals as well as nations.

> "They are called for adjudication pursuant to the Book of Allah." (*Al Omran* 23)

This means that functions of a prophet and that of government are inseparable.

> "No human, who Allah bestowed upon him the Book and governance and made him a prophet, will say to the people you must worship me and not worship Allah." (*Al Omran* 79)

Believing in Allah and His Messenger also requires believing in the Book.

> "Do believe in Allah, His Messenger and the Book." (*An-Nisa'* 136)

Muslims accept the People of the Book based on their common belief in Allah, and regardless of the particulars of their belief. The issue of the validity or invalidity of their beliefs may only be adjudicated by Allah.

> "Be gracious with the People of the Book when you debate them, unless they act oppressively. Say to them: We believe in what was sent down to us and what was sent down to you. Our god and your god are one and the same, and under Him we join the peace." (*Al-'Ankaboot* 46)

Al-Hujjat, Al-Furqan

Al-Hujjat means a very strong argument and/or evidence. *Al-Furqan* is the decisive evidence that distinguishes right from falsehood. *Al-Furqan* is a second name for Al-Quran because it provides the conclusive and perfect argument and evidence for Al-Islam.

> "Oh you people: You have received proof from your Lord." (*An-Nisa'* 174)

> "*Yaseen.* By Al-Quran you are one of the Messengers." (*Yaseen* 1–3)

> "We have a Book that speaks *Al-Haqq.*" (*Al-Mou'minoon* 62)

> "Allah has the perfect argument." (*Al-An'am* 149)

Al-Hudood

Al-Hudood is the plural of *had*. *Had* is the boundary, the border line that separates two or more things and may not be crossed. *Al-Mahdood* is the limited. The verb *yahud* means to limit, to check. Thus the essence of *had* is a line that is forbidden to be crossed. It sets the limit to what everyone may do in all freedom and innocence without fearing any punishment. *Al-Hudood* are an essential part, a backbone, of Al-Sharia.

In fact, *Al-Hudood* are the limits set by Allah to insure the full observance and application of Al-Sharia in order to do away with oppression and guarantee security, safety, and peace in the human society.

> "These are the bounds of Allah. Do not get close to them." (*Al-Baqarat* 187)

That is, do not cross those lines. For whoever crosses those lines commits an offense against Allah and His Prophet Muhammad.

> "Whoever crossed the bounds of Allah and His Messenger..." (*Al-Mujadalat* 5)

Al-Hudood are of two kinds. The first kind is what Muslims may or may not eat or drink. The second is about crimes against persons and property. These offenses are punished by enforcing the *had*, that is, "the penalty." The *haddad* is the prison keeper.

The bounds of Allah are one, but not the only, guarantee of the observance of Al-Sharia. The main guarantee lies in the voluntary observance of Al-Sharia by each and every Muslim through abstinence.

Judgment

Al-Quran is the book of judgment in that it spells out Al-Sharia. Conflicts are to be resolved on the basis of what is provided in Al-Quran.

> "They are called to the Book of Allah to adjudicate among them." (*Al Omran* 23)

> "Those who do not judge according to what Allah sent down are the disbelievers." (*Al-Maedat* 44)

> "We have sent down the Book to you by the power of *Al-Haqq* to sit in judgment among people." (*An-Nisa'* 105)

Section Two

SELECTIONS FROM AL-QURAN INTERPRETED

These selections consist of two whole but short *Suwar, Al-Fatiha* and *Al-Alaq,* and of one long *Ayat, Ayat Al-Kursi.* They were selected for two reasons: because they embody many of the basics of the message of Al-Islam and express the heart of Al-Sharia, and because of their sheer majestic beauty.

Chapter Four

SURAT AL-FATIHA

In the name of Allah, Ar-Rahman, Ar-Raheem

Glory is to Allah, Rab-al-Alameen, Ar-Rahman, Ar-Raheem, potentate of the day of account and judgment. We worship you and seek your support. Guide us to the straight path, the path of those upon whom you bestowed your blessings and bounties, not those who incurred wrath, or those who lost their way. (Ameen.)

Al-Fatiha is Chapter One of "Al-Quran. Like other *Suwar*, it is always recited beginning with the *Ayat*: "In the name of Allah, *Ar-Rahman, Al-Raheem,* which is commonly referred to as the *Basmallat. Al-Fatiha* as a whole is the most heavily recited chapter of Al-Quran. It is read or recited hundreds of millions of times a day all over the globe, both as part of the five daily *salawat* (individual or group formal prayer services) and on numerous other occasions.

Most English translations commonly translate the *Basmallat* as "most compassionate" for *Ar-Rahman* and "most merciful" for *Al-Raheem*. Some use "most gracious" for *Ar-Rahman*. These translations are inaccurate, however. *Ar-Rahman* and *Al-Raheem* have no equivalent in languages other than Arabic. Compassion and mercy make up only a tiny part of the meaning of *Al-Raheem*.

Al-Fatiha is derived from the root *fataha*, and so is *Al-Fattah*. *Al-Fattah* is one of the Good Names of Allah. *Al-Fattah* has all the keys; hence, He is the opener of all doors and the determiner of solutions to all conflicts.

> "Say: our Lord shall bring us together and open us to each other by *Al-Haqq* for he is the all-knowing opener." (*Saba'* 27)

So does *Surat Al-Fatiha*. It brings together the believers and makes them open to each other as commanded by Allah, *Al-Fattah*.

In Arabic, the word *muftah*, which means the key, is derived from the root *fataha*, which is the antonym of close. The key opens the door and a lot of other things. The Prophet said, "I have been given the keys of speech." Whenever something is uncovered, the Arabic word for it is *in-fataha*.

> "We opened the gates of *As-Sama*." (*Al-Qamar* 11)

I would not translate *As-Sama'* into "heaven" because this would be inaccurate. In Arabic the plural of *As-Sama'* is *As-Samawat*, which means the vast open spaces that engulf the various components of *Al-Alameen*, which are defined below. For the moment, the nearest English equivalent of *Al-Alameen* is universe or cosmos.

The first *Ayaat* of every *Surat* are called *fawateh*, the plural of *fatiha*—that is, the keys to the *Surat*. As a *Surat*, *Al-Fatiha* is the key to Al-Quran and the guide to the meaning of the other *Suwar*. Each of the few *Ayaat* of *Al-Fatiha* is a projection into the rest of Al-Quran, again playing the function of a key.

Ar-Rahman and *Al-Raheem*

Both *Ar-Rahman* and *Al-Raheem* are Good Names of Allah. Both are derived from the root *rahama*. Most translators of Al-Quran found them almost identical. So what is the wisdom of using them next to His name in what seems to be a repetition?

> "Allah has Good Names. Pray to Him by using them." (*Al-Araf 180*)

But the choice of these two particular names for use with the name of Allah leads to the conclusion that they carry different but complementary meanings of critical significance. After all, they were selected from among ninety-nine such Good Names.

Granted, all the qualities connoted in the ninety-nine Good Names fall within the meaning of the name Allah. They indeed express many of His attributes. But the qualities and connotations found in the words *Ar-Rahman* and *Ar-Raheem* take the pre-eminent position among the other qualities, just like the front position taken by the *imam* when he leads prayers.

True, certain linguists of the Arabic language defined *Rahman* as the ultimate *rahmat*, mercy. But it is in *Ar-Raheem* that we find the meaning of infinite *rahmat*. Charity and enlightenment are of the essence of *rahmat*.

> "Allah bestows his *rahmat* on whoever He wishes." (*Al-Baqarat* 105)

No wonder that the two Good Names *Ar-Rahman* and *Ar-Raheem* are so close, for they belong to the same Allah. Moreover, both are derived from the root *rahama*. But *Ar-Rahman* carries a meaning which is significantly more special and distinguishes it from *Ar-Raheem*, although they both flow from the same origin.

Ar-Rahman

Let us start with the Good Name *Ar-Rahman*. There is a consensus that the attributes it describes belong exclusively to Allah and may not be attributed to anyone else. There is no *Rahman* but Allah, and only Allah may be called *Rahman*. This is of the essence of the evidence of Allah's unity.

> "Say: Pray to Allah, or pray to *Ar-Rahman*. Whatever name you call Him with in prayer is one of His Good Names." (*Al-Isra'* 110)

So what is the meaning of *Ar-Rahman*?

In successive *Ayaat* of the *Surat Al-Hasher* (22, 23, 24, and 25), one can find a gradual escalation in describing the attributes of Allah:

> "He is Allah and there is no divinity but Him. He knows all, whether secret or revealed. He is *Ar-Rahman* and *Ar-Raheem*. He is Allah and there is no divinity but Him. He is the Holy Potentate, the Peace, the Protector, the Paramount, the Secure, the Compensator, and the Almighty. His standing is infinitely higher than what some associate Him with. He is Allah, the Creator, the Originator, and the Designer. He is called by His Good Names. All what is on Earth and in the *Samawat* praise His standing which is infinitely higher than what some associate Him with. He is the Secure and Wise Ruler and Judge."

We read in *Surat Al-Nisa'*:

> "To Allah belong all that is in *Samawat* and on Earth. Allah sur-

rounds and overwhelms everything."
(*An-Nisa'* 126)

By surrounding everything, Allah controls, preserves and protects all things.

> "To Allah belong the East and the West. Anywhere you turn, you face Allah." (*Al-Baqarat* 115)

> "To Allah belong the domain of *Samawat* and Earth and what is in between them." (*Surat Al-Ma-edat* 17)

> "His seat embraces the *Samawat* and Earth." (*Surat Al-Baqarat* 255)

> "Allah restrains *Samawat* and Earth lest they dissipate for they will dissipate if any one other than Him holds them." (*Surat Fatir* 42)

> "He disposes of the reins of *Samawat* and Earth." (*Surat Al-Shura* 13)

Ar-Rahman is synonymous with Allah, just like Allah is synonymous with Lord, *Rab*. Throughout *Surat Ar-Rahman*, *Ar-Rahman* is used as synonymous with Allah. This is also the case in many other *Ayaat*.

> "She said: I seek refuge from you with *Ar-Rahman*." (*Mariam* 18)

> "I made a vow of fasting to *Ar-Rahman*." (*Mariam* 26)

> "To Allah, then, belongs the Dominion by *Al-Haqq*." (*Al-Firqan* 26)

> "This is the promise of *Ar-Rahman*." (*Yaseen* 52)

The relationship of *Ar-Rahman* to *rahm*, which shares the same root *rahama*, is not a coincidence. In Arabic, *rahm* is the womb. It is the place where a fetus is enveloped, thrives, and enjoys love, emotional attachment, and protection from evil.

> "It is He who makes shapes in the womb." (*Al Omran* 6)

> "Allah surrounds and overwhelms everything." (*An-Nisa'* 126)

> "He originated *Samawat* and Earth." (*Al-Baqarat* 117)

The Prophet Muhammad said, "*Ar-rahm* is an intricate plantlet attached by Allah to the Throne."

In a human female the womb envelops the fetus, the unborn baby. What envelops the entire realm of the creation, the *Samawat* and earth, including mankind and all creatures, the cosmos, and hence the *Alameen*, is similar to *rahm*. *Rahman* is derived from the root *rahama*, like *atshan*, one who is thirsty, is derived from *atash*, thirst; or *ghad-*

ban, one who is furious, from *ghadab*, fury; or *irfan*, scholarship, from *arafa*; or *shaitan*, Satan, from *shatan*, mischief. Each of these examples describes a state, a condition, and its possessor.

Ar-Rahman is undoubtedly much greater and much more powerful than the creation He continues to bond, care for, and protect forever. The entire universe is engulfed in one *rahm* by the power of Allah. *Ar-Rahman* is the owner and possessor of this great cosmic *rahm*. When Allah is called by the Good Name *Ar-Rahman*, this expresses the limitless power of Allah and His care for what He originated, which is also limitless, including the universe and earth. The width and depth of the creation is not capable of being imagined:

> "Of a day that was equal to fifty thousand years." (*Al-Ma'arej* 42)

That is, fifty thousand years on earth are equal to one day in universal space under Allah.

Allah, also called *Ar-Rahman* or *Rab-al-Alameen* (definition to follow), envelops the earth and the universe. By this power and in this capacity, Allah:

(1) Originated and designed the universe.
(2) Envelops it.
(3) Controls it.
(4) Bonds, protects, and cares for it.

To avoid any farfetched interpretation of the above, reference is made to *Surat Al-Ikhlas*:

"Say Allah is one and the only one. Allah is eternal and He is the recourse. He did not bear children and He was not born. None was ever his equal."

Ar-Raheem

The Good Name *Ar-Raheem* represents the other facet of the infinite power of Allah. It is the object of the exercise of power. *Ar-Raheem* is the source of infinite *rahmat*, mercy. *Ar-Rahmat* is the generous grant without any consideration, or the expectation of any reciprocity, of all that is good, particularly welfare, security, peace, and love. It connotes the caring for all the creation and creatures with kindness, sympathy, charity, giving, and all that can be expressed in the meaning of grace and love.

> "My *rahmat* embraces everything." (*Al-Araf* 165)

> "Our Lord: You have embraced everything in your *rahmat* and knowledge." (*Ghafer* 7)

The quality of *Ar-Raheem* depicts caring, and all that arises from *rahmat* is called *ni'mat*, plural *ni'am*. The closest English translation of *ni'mat* is blessing and bounty.

> "We found room for him in our *rahmat*." (*Al-Anbiya'* 75)

The Prophet Muhammad said, "Allah's *rahmat* has room for everything."

"Glory be to Allah, *Rab-al-Alameen*"

Hamd means glory and is used exclusively to praise Allah. It is followed by an escalation in the use of the Good Names of Allah. He is *Rab-al-Alameen*. *Rab* is the lord to worship. *Alameen* is the plural of *alam* which, in the singular, literally means "the world." *Alameen* denotes the universe and every component thereof, including humans, animals, plants, and matter. *Rab-al-Alameen* is the Lord of everything. According to Muhib bin Munbih, Allah has eighteen thousand *alam* and Earth is only one of them.

Rab-al-Alameen is potentate of the day of account and judgment. He is also *Ar-Rahman, Ar-Raheem*.

"Potentate of the day of account and judgment"

Yaoum-ed-Deen means the day of account and judgment. "Account and judgment" is one of several meanings of the noun *deen*, which include religion, governance, and *sharia*. The day of account and judgment is the day of resurrection, when all souls are brought to account and are judged for what they did in their lifetime. But a human is also culpable and accountable during his lifetime, and the day he is tried and judged is also *yaoum-ed-deen*. In both cases, this day belongs to Allah. On the day of account and judgment, impartial justice is done through enforcing Al-Sharia and upholding the rule of law.

Al-Dayan is derived from the same root as *deen*. It is one of the Good Names of Allah. It means the highest judge or arbitrator. *Al-Dayan* also has the power of enforcing his judgments. This is dealt with under a separate heading.

"We worship you and seek your support"

To worship, *ya'bud*, is to submit and obey. *Al-Abd* is the worshipper. Allah is the worshipped, *Al-Ma'bood*. Based on this *Al-Abd/Al-Ma'bood* relationship, *Al-Abd* may seek aid and assistance from Allah. The purpose of this support is found in *al-Ayaat* to follow.

"Guide us to the straight path"

Assirat-tul-mustaqeem is the straight path for which guidance, *huda*, is sought.

Huda is the antonym of *dhalal*. The verb for this noun is *dhalla*, which means to stray. *Al-huda* means the wise choice. If one follows the footsteps of another, it is said that he is guided by his *huda*. Allah grants us *al-huda* to find the way.

> "Say: Allah guides to *Al-Haqq*." (*Younus* 35)
>
> "I have been guided by Allah to the straight path." (*Al-An'am* 161)

Al-Hadi, he who guides, is one of the Good Names of Allah.

The phrase "*Assirat-tul-mustaqeem*" is frequently employed in Al-Quran. It is synonymous with the "path of Allah." For example:

> "You are one of our messengers who are on the straight path." (*Yaseen* 4 and 5)
>
> "You shall be guided unto the straight path." (*Ash-Shura* 53)

Both of these *Ayaat* are addressed to the Prophet Muhammad.

> "Follow me on this straight path." (*Az-Zukhruf* 61)
>
> "Allah shall guide those who believe in Him unto the straight path." (*Al-Hajj* 55)
>
> "You shall summon them to the straight path." (*Al-Mou'minoon* 64)
>
> "Follow me and I shall lead you to the straight path." (*Mariam* 43)
>
> "You shall know who are on the straight path." (*Taha* 135)

There are many hypotheses as to the origin and meaning of the word *siratt*. Did it come from the Latin *strata*? Or does it have an Aramaic origin? Arab linguists defined *siratt* and *zirat* as "the way." Another possible origin of *siratt* is *satr*, with the inversion of the *r* and the *t*. *Satr* means a line in writing or a line of trees and the like. Still another possible origin is *shart*, which means condition or obligation. Perhaps all these meanings enter into the definition of *siratt*, which would be "the way or the line which one should follow."

"Straight" here is a translation of the Arabic *mustaqeem*. This word comes from the root *qawama* and its verbs are *qama*, *aqama*, and *estaqama*. It means to stand up, to make, to carry out, to take place, to play the character of, to persist in, to be steadfast, to have the duty to, to care for, and to be fair and just. It denotes an attachment to an act or action or something else taking place. *Al-qaim* of something is the one in charge of it. Allah is the *Al-Hay Al-Qayyoum*, which means the live one who is in charge. *Aqama assalat* means commenced prayers. *Al-qaim* of a right is the one observing it. *Al-qawam* is justice. *Al-qyam* is standing up. Following are a few *Ayaat* by way of illustration.

> "They stood up and said: our Lord is the Lord of *Samawat* and Earth." (*Akahf* 14)

> "Let the prayers commence." (*Hood* 114)

> "Oh you believers discharge your duty to Allah and give your testimony with justice." (*Al-Ma-edat* 9)

> "Be fair and just according to what you have been commanded." (*Hood* 113)

> "Be fair and just according to what you have been commanded and do not follow their whims…I am commanded to pass judgment justly among you. Allah is our Lord and yours. We are responsible for our deeds and you are responsible for yours. There should be no argument between you and us. Allah brings us together." (*Al-Shura* 15)

> "Those who said Allah is our Lord and are steadfast shall be in no peril and will not grieve." (*Al-Ihqaq* 14)

> "Allah made *Al-Qaabah* an inviolable Holy House so that humans shall be steadfast." (*Al-Maedat* 97)

> "Stand up for the true creed." (*Ar-Room* 43)

The Prophet Muhammad said, "Say 'I believe in Allah,' and be fair and just."

What is the straight path? It is the body of principles and other prescribed directions for conduct and action, rules.

> "We have prescribed for each of you *Sher'aton* and process." (*Al-Ma-edat* 48)

The Arabic verb *shara'a* (in the past tense) means legislated.

> "He legislated for you what He commanded Noah to observe." (*Al-Shura* 13)

The noun *sher'aton* is the singular of *Sharia*. "Process" is a translation from the Arabic *manhaj*, derived from the root *nahaja*, which means the way. It is suggested that the *manhaj* is the straight path. It is also suggested that *Sheraton* and process are the way and tradition, i.e., the Sunnat, of the Prophet Muhammad.

In Arabic the word *shari'* means simply the broadest avenue. The right way is the broadest avenue. It is the message of Islam, a master plan based, from both the religious and the legal points of view, on justice, enforcing right, upholding the rule of the rules that have legitimate sources, peace, charity, and love. Among its banners one may find Allah's words:

> "The needy and the underprivileged have a definite right in the riches of the wealthy." (*Al-Ma'arej* 20)

> "So that [wealth] will not revolve exclusively among those of you who are rich…" (*Al-Hasher* 8)

The Prophet Muhammad said, "Unholy is the nation that does not take from the powerful to give to the weak."

The *Ayaat* are full of descriptions of the content of this path, such as its subjects and objectives. For example:

> "It is Allah's command to do justice and good, to fulfill one's duties to his relatives and to refrain from indulgence, scantiness and wrongdoing. He so exhorts you so that you will keep it in mind." (*Al-Nahl* 90)

> "They are the ones who repent, worship and glorify Allah, recognize that His standing is infinitely higher than what some associate Him with, bow and kneel before Him, command goodness and forbid wrongdoing, and observe the bounds He set." (*Al-Tawbat* 112)

> "The believers, male and female, guard each other, command goodness and forbid wrongdoing." (*Al-Tawbat* 71)

> "Do your duty and give to the relative what he is due, and to the poor and the traveling their rights." (*Al-Room* 39)

> "The weak, the sick, and those who cannot find money to spend from, shall not suffer." (*Al-Tawbat* 91)

"The path of those upon whom you bestowed your blessings and bounties, not those who incurred wrath, or those who lost their way"

The straight path leads to all that is right and just, and Allah's guidance is prayed for to make the believers part of the group of humans upon whom He bestowed His bounties, and not part of those who brought wrath upon themselves for having breached their commitment to Al-Islam:

> "If they breach their faith after having made their covenant..." (*Al-Tawbat* 9)

or those who strayed although they could see the straight path:

> "Allah shall make you see [the straight path] so that you do not stray." (*Al-Nisa'* 176)

> "Those who stray from the path of Allah..." (*Saadd* 26)

It is unlikely that any People of the Book are specifically targeted by the phrase "incurred wrath" or the phrase "lost their way," as is known to be popular in some quarters.

Al-Fatiha addresses *Rab Al-Alameen*, the Lord of all the worlds, not just the Muslim population. Allah is not only Lord of the Muslims, but also of the People of the Book and of all of humankind. He is Lord of the Universe and all beings.

> "On the Day of Judgment Allah shall adjudicate between the believers, the Jews, the Sabians, the Christians, the Magians, and the polytheists." (*Al-Hajj* 17)

> "Be gracious with the People of the Book when you debate them, unless they act oppressively. Say to them: We believe in what was sent down to us and sent down to you. Our god and your god are one and the same, and under Him we join the peace." (*Al-'Ankaboot* 46)

> "You will find those who say: We are Christians, to have the most regard [to Muslims]." (*Al-Maedat* 82)

Al-Islam does not recognize collective responsibility. It only upholds individual responsibility arising from what every human being does, whether good or evil, in the exercise of his own independent will. "No human may be credited with more than his own upside. No burdened human shall bear the burden of another burdened human" (*Al-An'am* 164).

Hence the measure of holding individuals to having "incurred wrath" or "lost their way" is not through their religion but their own deeds.

> "An atheist is responsible for his own atheism. Whoever does a good deed

> makes a provision for himself." (*Ar-Room* 44)

> "Every human shall be recompensated with what he earned." (*Al-Jathiat* 22)

Al-Quran provides that there are the good and the bad among People of the Book.

> "There are those People of the Book who could be trusted with a treasure of gold and others who could not be trusted with one dinar." (*Al Omran* 75)

The steadfast *ummat,* the best translation of which is nation, is the one that is steadfast and firm in holding to the articles of its creed. Hence there are People of the Book who deserve praise.

> "The People of the Book include among them those who believe in Allah and what was sent down to you and sent down to them. They bow humbly before Allah." (*Al Omran* 199)

Ameen

This word is not part of the *Surat* but is recited at its end to offer and confirm one's acknowledgment, support, and acceptance of and agreement to the contents of the *Surat* and to ask Allah to accept the prayer embodied in it.

The Covenant

In short, the *Surat* of *Al-Fatiha* summarizes the covenants between Allah and his worshippers which gave rise to a *meethaqq*, a compact, which is a confirmed covenant.

> "Those who fulfill their covenant with Allah and do not violate the compact [are the believers]." (*Al-Raad* 20)

On their side of *Al-Meethaqq*, the worshippers persist faithfully in obeying and loving Allah and in glorifying and thanking Him for all the bounties He bestowed upon them. They follow the straight path and look to Allah to guide them to it. The straight path is their avenue to the realization of *rahmat* and love among themselves both as individuals and as groups. They uphold and obligate themselves to the Islamic message both as a belief and as Al-Sharia.

> "Muhammad the Messenger of Allah and his companions are stout against the dis-believers, but tender among each other." (*Al-Fateh* 29)

Violating *Al-Meethaqq* is offensive and brings upon the violator a great penalty.

> "They are losers those who break their covenant with Allah after it became a compact and sever what

Allah commanded to be joined." (*Al-Baqarat* 27)

This mission did not commence with the Prophet's message but was started by prior prophets going all the way back to Ibrahim:

> "Say: Allah has showed me the straight path, a steadfast way for the people of Ibrahim." (*Al-Anaam* 161)

> "We sent our messengers so that each preached in the language of his people....The messengers said to their people: do you doubt the existence of Allah who created *Samawat* and Earth?" (*Ibrahim* 10)

> "Say: we believe in Allah and what has been revealed to us and what was revealed to Ibrahim." (*Al-Baqarat* 136)

> "As Ibrahim was raising the foundations of the House with Ismail, he prayed: Allah, please accept this from us. You verily listen and you are the most knowledgeable. Allah, make us submit to you as Muslims and make our descendants Muslim....Allah said to him: become a Muslim and he said I joined the peace under *Rab-al-Alameen*." (*Al-Baqarat* 127)

> "He [Ibrahim] said: I am the first of the Muslims." (*Al-Anaam* 163)

More simply stated, Allah, *Ar-Rahman*, created, protected, and enabled *Al-Alameen* to thrive, like a human embryo thrives in the womb of his mother. He granted His *Rahmat* to all His creatures. His *Rahmat* materialized lovingly in the form of the various bounties that He bestowed upon them. It is the role of humans to jointly maintain the existence and flow of these bounties with love among themselves by observing the principles and rules of Al-Sharia through the straight path.

Chapter Five

SURAT AL-ALAQ

In the name of Allah, Ar-Rahman, Ar-Raheem

Read in the name of your Lord who created. He created the human being by implantation. Read! Your most generous Lord teaches by the pen, teaching the human being what he did not know. The human being tends, upon self-enrichment, to be oppressive. Yet authority rests with your Lord. Have you seen the one who disputed our subject [Muhammad] while praying? Have you known the one who is rightly guided and preaching abstinence from evil deeds? Have you not seen the one who lied and turned away? Did he not know that Allah watches? If he does not desist, we will slap him on the forehead, a lying and sinful forehead. Let him call his fellow councilmen. We will call the attendants of hell fire. No, heed him not, bow down in prayer and come closer.

The *Ayaat* of this *Surat* were revealed in two stages. The first five *Ayaat* came in first stage in the Mecca period—i.e., prior to the *Hijrat*—and are, as to order, the earliest five *Ayaat* of Al-Quran.

"Read!"

This verb has a distinctive meaning which is fully discussed above under the subtitle "Al-Quran."

"In the name of your Lord"

That is, by the will of Allah.

"Who created. He created the human being"

"The human being" is our best translation of the Arabic noun *al-insan*, the plural of which is *an-nas*. This term is gender neutral. It is used in contrast to English, French, and other European languages that have no equivalent term. The French Declaration of the Rights of Man and the Citizen uses the noun "man," and so does the United States' Declaration of Independence.

Allah created the human being and everything else.

"By implantation"

"Implantation" is our best translation of the Arabic *alaq*. Its literal meaning is attachment; its best meaning is love. In the present tense the verb from this noun is *yalaq*, which means to cling or attach to. A woman is said to be *aleqat*, the same verb but in the past tense, when she becomes pregnant.

"Read!"

This is a reconfirmation of the order to read.

"Your most generous Lord teaches by the pen"

Knowledge is preserved and transmitted by writing through the use of a pen. Allah is very generous in making knowledge available to human beings through teaching. In Al-Islam knowledge is a great *ni'mat*, blessing, bounty.

"Teaching the human being what he did not know"

The first aim of the message is to eradicate ignorance. The era that preceded Al-Islam is called *Al-Jahelia*, coined from *jahl*, which means ignorance. By learning what Allah has to teach him through Al-Quran, a human being is able to cross over from the era of *Al-Jahelia* to the era of knowledge.

The next group of *Ayaat* describes an incident representative of the confrontation with the era of *Al-Jahelia* that was going on in the early period of the Prophet Muhammad's message in Mecca and led eventually to his migration to Al-Madina with most of his followers, the *Hijrat*. In this story, one of the uncles of the Prophet, referred to as *Abou Jahl*, who was also his fiercest opponent, approached him while he was praying in the sanctuary and attempted to dissuade him from going through with his prayers.

"The human being tends, upon self-enrichment, to be oppressive"

Knowledge is not acquired with riches and the abundance of servants but only with learning. But *Abou Jahl* did not think so, and his riches and stature as a member of the Mecca Council enabled him to be oppressive. This was the state of affairs in *Al-Jahelia*. The state of oppression, *zulm*, is the opposite of the state of peace. Comprehensive peace is one of the high goals of Al-Islam. What the Prophet received from his uncle was pure *zulm*.

"Have you seen the one who disputed our subject [Muhammad] while praying?"

This is a reference to the attempt of *Abou Jahl* to confront the Prophet Muhammad while in the act of praying in order to dissuade him from completing his prayers.

"Have you known the one who is rightly guided and preaching abstinence from evil deeds?"

This is a reference to the Prophet Muhammad, who is rightly guided and preaches *taqwa*, abstinence from evil deeds and observance of Al-Sharia.

"Have you not seen the one who lied and turned away?"

The reference is to *Abou Jahl* who, after unsuccessfully disputing the Prophet Muhammad, turned away and fled in fear of the possible consequences of his interference.

"Yet authority rests with your Lord"

Abou Jahl was not aware that Allah had the upper authority. This is a reference to Al-Sharia, which must be observed. Human beings will be brought to account for any violation of Al-Sharia.

"If he does not desist, we will slap him on the forehead"

This is a warning to the oppressor. It leaves the door open for him to repent and receive forgiveness.

"Lying and sinful forehead"

This is a description of the oppressor, a lying sinner.

"Let him call his fellow councilmen. We will call the attendants of hell fire!"

The source of *Abou Jahl*'s power was his supporters who sat on the Mecca Council, which gathered together regularly at the meeting hall, *Dar-al-Nadwa*. *Abou Jahl* is warned that the Prophet Muhammad is under the protection of Allah. If *Abou Jahl* calls his fellow councilmen to support his transgressions against the Prophet, the attendants of Hell Fire, *Al-Zabania*, will deal with them.

"No, heed him not, bow down in prayer and come closer"

This commands the Prophet not to give in to oppression and to continue his prayers by bowing down and coming closer to Allah.

Chapter Six

AYAT AL-KURSI

In the name of Allah, Ar-Rahman, Ar-Raheem

Allah, who there is no divinity but Him, is the Giver and the Sustainer of life. He could not be corrupted or changed and He does not rest. All that is in As-Samawat or on Earth belong to Him. No one may intercede with Him to forgive someone else except with His leave. He has knowledge of everyone's present and past. No one may comprehend any of His knowledge unless He so wills. His chair is so wide as to embrace As-Samawat and Earth, and it does not burden him to hold them harmless. He is the most exalted and the most splendid.

Kursi means chair. *Ayat Al-Kursi* is part of *Surat Al-Baqarat (Ayat* 255), which is the longest *Surat* of Al-Quran and was revealed in the Al-Madina era, i.e., post-*Hijrat. Ayat Al-Kursi* is the second-most revered and -most recited *Ayat* of Al-Quran after

Surat Al-Fatiha. Its significance stems from its beauty, clarity, and its ability to inspire a feeling of safety and peace in the heart of its reader or reciter. There is no question that it is one of the greatest *Ayaat* of Al-Quran.

"The Giver"

This is our best translation from the Arabic *hay*. This is the adjective of the noun *hayat*, which means life. This is one literal meaning that cannot be applied to Allah, for he does not receive but gives life. When a *muazen* summons Muslims to prayer, he uses the phrase *Hayee Alas-Salat*. Here *hayee* means to give life to prayers. The often-used phrase *ihya-ul-lail* means staying up all night, thereby giving life to the night.

Whoever gives life owns. One who reclaims unproductive land and makes it fertile is said to have *ahya* such land, i.e., given it life.

"The Sustainer"

This is our best translation from the Arabic *Al-Qayyoum*. It comes from the root *qawama*. *Al-qyam* comes from the same root and its literal meaning is "getting up." The verb in the past tense is *qama*. If a right is proven, it is said to have stood up, *qama*. Another verb from the same root is *yuqeemu*. It means to construct, to cause to stand up like in building, to cause things to happen. *Al-Qayyoum* is Allah, who raised everything—that is, caused everything to stand up, to exist, and in short, to happen. Standing alone with no help from others, He sustains and cares for all.

Al-Qayyoum also means the just. Another derivative of the root *qawama* is *al-istiqamat*, which means standing justly. It also means believing in Allah as the one and only god. Finally, *Al-Qyamat* means resurrection. On the day thereof, *Youm-ul-Qyamat*, Allah raises all from the dead and brings them to account and judgment.

"He could not be corrupted or changed and He does not rest"

"Corruption and change" is our best translation from the Arabic *sinat*. We translated the Arabic *nawm*, whose literal meaning is "sleep," into "rest," which implies a motionless state and provides a deeper meaning. Allah does not rest but always stays fully alert, giving his creation His full attention.

"All that is in the Heavens or on Earth belong to Him"

This is a statement of truth.

"No one may intercede with Him to forgive someone else except with His leave"

In this context, interceding with Allah to forgive someone else is the meaning of the Arabic noun *al-shafa'at*. Forgiveness is sought for those who committed offenses under Al-Sharia or other violations of Islamic commandments. A third party may intercede through a *dua'a*, an earnest speech imploring Allah to do something such as forgive an offender. Such an act is not acceptable unless it has the prior authority of Allah. The Prophet Muhammad alone has such advance authority. In principle, *al-shafa'at* is not admissible for those who did not believe in the unity of Allah, including the Prophet's own parents.

"He has knowledge of the present and the past of everyone"

Allah has knowledge of everything and everyone in the past and present on an ongoing basis.

"No one may comprehend any of His knowledge unless He so wills"

Humans are infinitely less knowledgeable than Allah. Allah decides how much knowledge they may acquire.

"His chair embraces As-Samawat and Earth"

"Chair" is our best translation from the Arabic *kursi*. Its literal meaning is that thing which is structured and held together firmly. Hence Allah's chair is characteristic of the ability and power to give structure and hold firmly. The statement that Allah's chair is wide enough and large enough to embrace all *Samawat* and all earth describes His ability and power to give structure and hold *As-Samawat* and earth within His chair.

"It does not burden Him to hold them harmless"

The purpose of including As-*Samawat* and earth within Allah's chair is to preserve and protect them, to hold them harmless. This does not burden Him.

"He is the most ascending and the splendid"

This is a statement of truth when applied to Allah.

Section Three

CREED: MEANING BELIEF AND CHARITY

Chapter Seven

THE MEANING OF CREED

"Creed" is our best translation from the Arabic *deen*. Creed is a set of fundamental authoritative beliefs and guiding principles. *Deen* is usually translated into English as "religion." We firmly submit that the English term religion, and similar terms in French and other European languages, are not synonymous with the Arabic term *deen*. *Deen* is much closer in meaning to "creed," which means a set of fundamental authoritative beliefs and guiding principles.

Religion, on the other hand, is synonymous with the Arabic term *ibadat*, which means ideas and practices indicative of and displaying adherence to a certain worship of one or more deities. The conflict of definitions is the source of unwarranted confusion in the interpretation of the concept of separation of church and state with reference to Christianity and Al-Islam. Such separation comes naturally in the context of the history of relations between Christian churches and the state. Christianity was founded and grew in the shadow of strong empires. The eventual reconciliation between the two sides necessitated an assurance by Christian churches that they had no intention of interfering in the affairs of state. This became a reformist political position by politicians who wanted to make sure that the clergy would not weigh in with their influence over much of the masses.

None of this is true for Al-Islam. Al-Islam was founded on and grew in confrontation with empires. It has no church or clergy. Furthermore, it is a creed that does not confine itself to *al-ibadat* and the worship of Allah. Praying to Allah is a very significant part of Al-Islam, but is not the only part.

The Arabic word *deen* has many meanings, prime among which are:

(1) Belief in Allah, His Books, and Messengers without distinction. This belief is in the heart *and* is expressed by word of mouth.

> "The believers are those who believed in Allah and His Messenger and then they developed no doubts." (*Al-Hujurat* 15)

Partial belief is incomplete and inadequate.

> "Each of the believers believes in Allah, His angles, His Books, and His Messengers and does not distinguish between them." (*Al-Baqarat* 285)

> "Those who believe in what was sent down to you and what was sent down before you..." (*Al-Baqarat* 4)

Belief in the earlier messages and in the prophets who preceded the Prophet Muhammad is an integral part of Islamic belief. Someone who denies Jesus or Moses cannot be a Muslim.

> "Those who do not believe in Allah and His Messengers, wish to drive a wedge between Allah and His Messengers, or say we believe in some of them and deny the others, are the real atheists." (*An-Nisa'* 150–152)

(2) Worship of Allah, submitting to His will, and believing in His unity.

> "Say I have been commanded to worship Allah and to dedicate my creed to Him." (*Az-Zumar* 11)

> "Oh you people, worship your Lord who created you." (*Al-Baqarat* 21)

> "Show your faces in every mosque and pray to Him with dedication." (*Al-Araf* 29)

(3) Good character such as piety, honesty, charity, caring, loyalty, and humility.

"You do not attain devoutness by facing east or west, but by believing in Allah, the Last Day, the angels, the Books and the prophets, by giving the money you cherish to close relatives, orphans, the poor, the homeless travelers, those who beg for it, and to liberate slaves, by holding prayers, by giving *Zakat*, by fulfilling the promises you covenant, and by being steadfast in adversity, misfortune and calamity. Such are the people who speak the truth and observe abstinence." (*Al-Baqarat* 177)

"Do not touch the property of the orphan." (*Al-Isra'* 34)

"Oh you believers do not nullify your donations to charity by showing off or causing harm." (*Al-Baqarat* 264)

"Your Lord commanded that you worship Him alone and to be charitable to your parents." (*Al-Isra'* 23)

"Do not squander your money. Squanderers are the brothers of Satan." (*Al-Isra'* 26-27)

(4) Obedience to duties and binding obligations as commanded by Al-Sharia. This applies to civilian transactions in which one party becomes

obligated to other parties to do or to deliver something.

(5) Sovereignty.
This is power, dominance, rule, and ability to force and coerce.

(6) Judgment and justice.
The judge or arbiter is called *Ad-Dayan*. Allah is the supreme *Dayan*. The verb in the present tense is *yudeen*, which means to convict.

(7) Recompensation through penalty and reward.

(8) Accounting.
Youm-ud-deen is the day of account upon resurrection, the Day of Judgment. The one who does the accounting is *Al-Haseeb*. *Al-Haseeb* is one of the Good Names of Allah.

The inability of Western scholars and orientalists to understand proper and complete meaning of the Arabic *deen* has led them to commit grave errors in comparing Al-Islam in its entirety to Christianity. Consequently, they deemed Al-Sharia to be mere religious law, which did not exist in their own cultures. As a result, they waged a campaign to strike down Al-Sharia or limit its sphere of application, a position supported by their equally confused governments.

Chapter Eight

CREED: MEANING BELIEF

The pillars of Al-Islam are stated in the context of belief, *al-eeman*. They are five in number, namely: the testimony that there is no divinity but Allah and that Muhammad is His Messenger; praying; fasting; giving *Zakat*; and, if possible, making the pilgrimage to Allah's sanctuary in Mecca. In addition, Al-Islam particularly reveres seven good characteristics or traits, namely: *taqwa*, abstinence; *mahabbat*, loving; *birr*, devoutness; *nazahat*, integrity; *zimmat*, devotedness and loyalty; *fadeelat*, virtue; and *ihsan*, charity. Together with the Pillars of Al-Islam, they constitute the essence of the creed, meaning belief.

Abstinence

Taqwa is derived from *al-weqayat*, which is building a barrier between a Muslim and what is offensive. It means abstaining from everything that is offensive, evil, or violates the belief and Al-Sharia. The opposite of *taqwa* is *ithm*, wickedness.

> "The most abstinent among you is the most highly regarded by Allah." (*Al-Hujurat* 13)

> "Cooperate with each other in devoutness and abstinence, but not in wickedness and aggression." (*Al-Maedat* 2)

> "Be just. That is closer to abstinence." (*Al-Maedat* 8)

Loving

Al-mahabbat is a condition of being a believer. One who cannot love cannot believe.

The Prophet Muhammad said, "By Allah you will not enter Paradise until you believe, and you will not believe until you love each other."

The Loving is one of the Good Names of Allah.

Devoutness

Al-birr is best translated as devoutness and to a lesser extent as piety. It is the state of being honest, good, benevolent, kind, gentle, and charitable with all persons, and observant of Islamic duties in worship and under Al-Sharia. The opposite of *birr* is *ouqooq*.

"You will not attain devoutness unless you spend from what you cherish." (*Al Omran* 92)

"You may not command people to be devout and forget yourselves." (*Al-Baqarat* 44)

Integrity

Nazahat means staying away from corruption. It implies wholeness and the absence of defects. *Tanzeeh* is used to mean denying or refuting the false allegations of infidels against Allah.

Devotedness

Zimmat is loyalty and devotedness. It is the state of refraining from violating what is sacred and falls under Allah's protection, *al-hurumat*, such as in covenants and peace. *Hurumat* is sanctity. The *zimmat* is not individual but collective to all Muslims. Muslims share one *zimmat*.

Virtue

Fadeelat is moral excellence characterized by charity, goodness, and dignity.

"Allah has the greatest virtue." (*Al-Baqarat* 105)

Because Allah has the greatest virtue, every Muslim should learn about the virtues attributed to

Allah and of which His Good Names are descriptive, such as being merciful, generous, and forgiving.

Charity

Al-ihsan is first due to one's father and mother. This is the most cherished virtue and a moral and Al-Sharia obligation.

> "Allah commands that you worship Him and only Him and that you be charitable to your parents." (*Al-Isra'* 23)

Next, it is due to close relatives and relatives in general. Next, it is due to neighbors. Next, it is due to friends, the poor and the orphans, travelers who have no place to stay, and the homeless.

The duty of giving charity to one's neighbors arises from social solidarity among Muslims, but charity may also apply to a non-Muslim neighbor. The Prophet Muhammad said, "Your polytheist neighbor is still your neighbor and he has the right of a neighbor. If your neighbor is Muslim he has the right of a neighbor and the right of a Muslim. If your neighbor is a Muslim and he is your relative then he has the rights of a neighbor, a Muslim and a relative."

Chapter Nine

THE GOOD NAMES OF ALLAH

A name in Arabic is *ism*, plural *asma'*. It is a sign, an indication, of the person or thing and his, her, or its attributes. It also indicates language and meaning. The Good Names, *al-asma' al-husna*, of Allah are names and adjectives used for Allah in Al-Quran. They embody various attributes of Allah according to human comprehension.

> "He taught Adam all the names." (*Al-Baqarat* 31)

Ninety-nine such Good Names have been listed, but there may be more. Each of them sets a high example for Muslims to be inspired by or try to follow as a high role model of ideal character.

Ar-Rahman: *Ar-Rahman* is a name unique to and synonymous with Allah.

Ar-Raheem: *Ar-Raheem* is the source of infinite *rahmat*, mercy.

The Potentate: *Al-Malek* is the potentate over the universe and all things therein.

The Holy: *Al-Qaddous* is the holy.

The Peace: *As-Salam*, the peace.

The Giver of Security and Faith: *Al-Mu'min*. He is the giver and source of security, faith, and confidence.

The Guardian: *Al-Muhaimin*. He watches over. By Him the message of Al-Islam not only reconfirms but also supersedes earlier messages of Allah.

> "We have sent down to you the book by the power of *Al-Haqq* confirming what He holds of, and superseding, the [earlier] books." (*Al-Ma-edat* 48)

The Almighty: *Al-Azeez* is the unassailable, the invincible, because He is stronger than anything and everything. *Izzat* is the noun which means an intense sense of invincibility, well-being, and importance.

The Mender: *Al-Jabbar* is the one who frees from faults and defects, and who puts into good order something that was damaged or injured.

The Magisterial: *Al-Mutakabber* is the master marked with overbearing dignity and authority.

The Creator: *Al-Khaliq* is the giver of life.

The Maker: *Al-Bari'* creates humans in a state of innocence and grants clemency.

The Determiner: *Al-Musawwer* is the willing, the decision maker, the shaper of destinies, looks, and genes.

The All-Protector: *Al-Ghaffar* is the protector of the universal system.

The Coercer: *Al-Qah-har* is the dominant subduer who uses coercion to enforce his commands and judgments.

The Endower: *Al-Wah-hab* is the giver of a notable capacity, power, talent, quality, attribute, or physical asset.

The Provider: *Al-Razzaq* insures that all the creatures of Allah fall upon the means of maintaining their livelihood.

Keeper of the Keys: *Al-Fattah* has all the keys; hence He is the opener of all doors and the determiner of solutions to all conflicts. A judge is also called *Fattah*. *Al-Fateh* is water unlocked from springs.

> "We opened for them the doors of everything." (*Al-An'am* 44)

The All-Knowing: *Al-Aleem* has all and absolute knowledge.

> "He knows everything." (*Al-Baqarat* 29)

The Taker: *Al-Qabidd* restricts, constrains, or takes away, such as in death.

The Extender: *Al-Bassett* reaches out, stretches, and expands.

The Abater: *Al-Khafed* diminishes the offenders upon the Day of Judgment, beats them down, or puts an end to their actions.

The Exalter: *Al-Mou'izz* is he who brings about *izzat*, an intense sense of invincibility, well-being, and importance.

The Humbler: *Al-Muzill* humbles or brings about *zull*, an intense state of humiliation, shame, humbleness, lessened rank in society, and/or degradation.

The All-Hearing: *As-Samee'* attentively hears all.

The All-Seeing: *Al-Baseer* attentively sees all.

The Adjudicator: *Al-Hakam* is the judge, arbiter.

> "He will then adjudicate among us by *Al-Haqq*." (*Saba'* 26)

The Justice: *Al-Adl* is the just and justice.

The Deliverer: *Al-Lateef* gently saves from harm or injury. Its root, *latafa*, is the opposite of violence.

The All-Proficient: *Al-Khabeer* has all the knowledge of all skills and doings.

The Magnanimous: *Al-Haleem* is forbearing, deals with offenses calmly, displays noble generosity, disdains meanness, and does not rush to react.

The Splendid: *Al-Azeem* is limitlessly extensive and huge, with such unlimited magnitude that it defies human comprehension of His nature.

The Forgiving: *Al-Ghafoor* is the one who grants forgiveness for offenses, pardons, and covers errors and faults.

The Rewarder: *Ash-Shakoor* appreciates good deeds and reciprocates with generous rewards.

The Most Exalted: *Al-Aliy* is the one who is high in place, outstanding, having transcendent excellence and inspiring awe. Allah is most often mentioned as Allah *ta-ala*, which is the verb of the noun *Aliy*. Part of the intent is to absolve Him from assertions or descriptions that embody or imply *shurk*.

The Great: *Al-Kabeer* is the one remarkable and predominant.

The Preserver: *Al-Hafeez* is the one who holds, maintains, and protects.

The Nourisher: *Al-Muqeet* is the provider of subsistence, the conditions of remaining in existence.

The Counter: *Al-Haseeb* sets the accounts of human beings on the day of reckoning.

The Absolute: *Al-Jaleel* is the perfect and has no restriction, qualification, or exception. The noun *Jalal* can only be used in connection with Allah: *Allah Jalla Jalaluhu.*

The Generous: *Al-Kareem* is the one characterized with generosity.

The Watchful: *Ar-Raqeeb* is the overseer and protector.

The Responsive: *Al-Mujeeb* responds to prayers and calls for assistance.

The Spacious: *Al-Wa-se'* is the one who has unlimited space for his mercy and endowments.

> "My *rahmat* is vast and inclusive of everything." (*Al-A'araf* 156)

The Learned: *Al-Hakeem* is the wise, learned, and just judge.

The Loving: *Al-Wadood.*

The Resplendent: *Al-Majeed* is the glorious one who shines with charity, generosity, and honor.

The Resurrector: *Al-Ba'eth* is the one who raises the dead.

The Witness: *Ash-Shaheed* is the conclusive witness.

The Right: *Al-Haqq* is what is proven, valid, and true, admitting of no doubt, firmly established, the opposite of oppression, the source of all rules.

The Trustee: *Al-Wakeel* the one who is in charge and manages the affairs of humans better than they can manage them themselves.

The Powerful: *Al-Qaweey* is the strongest one, the most capable.

The Robust: *Al-Mateen* is strongly formed and fully bodied; full of strength, firmness, and vigor; and tireless.

The Assistance Provider: *Al-Waleey* helps and supports, as a matter of right and duty, all those who need His help and support.

The Glorified: *Al-Hameed* is the most praiseworthy, the one to whom Muslims say glory as often as possible, *Al-Hamdu lil-Lah*, for no specific reason or in response to all events and incidents.

The Evaluator: *Al-Muhsee* is the one who appreciates the merits based on all-encompassing knowledge.

The Creative: *Al-Mubdi'* is the one who makes new creations or inventions that are not based on earlier models.

The Restarter: *Al-Mu'eed* starts and restarts creation and finally reclaims all.

> "He starts creation, restarts it, and, finally, to Him you shall return." (*Ar-room* 11)

The Reviver: *Al-Muhyee* brings about, or restores, life.

The Closer: *Al-Mumeet* brings life to an end.

The Giver of Life: *Al-Hayee* does not receive but gives life and lives forever.

The Sustainer: *Al-Qayyoum* takes care of the living.

The Finder: *Al-Wajid* looks for and finds knowledge, acts, finds results, succeeds, and receives inexhaustible riches.

The Dignified: *Al-Majed* has the qualities of distinction, rank, honor, and generosity.

The One and Only: *Al-Wahid* is the one who is not capable of being subdivided, has no equal, and does not take associates.

The Eternal: *As-Samadd* is immortal, free from want and needs but is capable of fulfilling all the wishes and needs of His worshippers.

The Potent: *Al-Qader* is of intensive power, value, knowledge, means, and ability.

The Absolute Power: *Al-Muqtader* yields absolute and irresistible power.

The Expediter: *Al-Muqaddem* brings gifts closer.

The Retarder: *Al-Mouakh-kher* causes reduction of speed without actually stopping.

The First: *Al-Aw-wal* is the one who always existed from the eternity, the very first to exist.

The Last: *Al-Akher* is the one whose existence has no end.

The Apparent: *Az-Zaher* is openly, clearly, and manifestly evident to those who believe in Him.

The Out of Sight: *Al-Baten* is he who is hidden, invisible, concealed, and who knows all secrets.

The Authoritative: *Al-Wali* is the holder of power, authority.

The Ascending: *Al-Muta-ali* is the one of supreme highness.

The Devouted: *Al-Barr* is the one who is honest, good, benevolent, kind, gentle, and charitable.

The Judge of Repentance: *At-Tawab* receives and examines, accepts acts of true repent, and, as a result, forgives.

The Punitive: *Al-Muntaqem* imposes and enforces punishment for wrongdoing.

The Pardoner: *Al-Afouw* excuses an offense or releases the penalty of the guilty.

The Sympathizer: *Ar-Raouf* is the one with tender and merciful concern for others who find themselves in a condition of distress or misery and shares their feelings and assists with the removal of this condition.

Master of the Realm: *Malek Al-Mulk* owns the kingdom of As-Samawat and earth.

Characterized with Perfection and Generosity: *Zu Al-Jalali Wal-Ikram* is the one who is perfect in every way.

The Upright: *Al-Muqasset* is one with strict sense of balance and fairness.

The Constitutor: *Al-Jame'* makes compositions of many ingredients.

The Self-Sufficient: *Al-Ghaney* has no needs, but everyone needs Him.

The Enricher: *Al-Moughni* enriches whomever He pleases.

The Immuner: *Al-Mani'* provides and protects immunity.

The Injurious: *Ad-Darr* inflicts harm either in preparation for doing good or in enforcing rights, doing justice, or applying penalties.

The Benevolent: *An-Nafe'* is conducive to all that is good and favorable.

The Shining Light: *An-Noor* stands for right, knowledge, evidence, and guidance.

The Leader: *Al-Hadi* guides and directs the way.

The Originator: *Al-Badi'* creates from nothing and according to no existing model.

The Everlasting: *Al-Baqi* is the eternal.

The Receiver: *Al-Wareth* is the one who reclaims everyone and everything, and He is their final recourse.

The Patient: *As-Saboor* is the one who is not rash and does not rush to action.

The Wise: *Ar-Rasheed* guides to the right course through reason.

Section Four

CREED: MEANING AL-HAQQ AND AL-SHARIA

Chapter Ten

AL-HAQQ

It is already established that creed is more than just religion in the Western or Christian meaning. The other part of the creed of Al-Islam consists mainly of *Al-Haqq* and *Al-Sharia.*

The closest English word for the Arabic *Al-Haqq* is "the right." The basic meaning of *Al-Haqq* is that which is right, evident, true, and obliging, but it has many more specific meanings. *Ibn Al-Atheer* defines *Al-Haqq* as that which truly exists, whose existence has been verified, and always exists without defect or corruption.

Allah is *Al-Haqq.* In this meaning, *Al-Haqq* is the origin of all existence and both the fountain of the message of Al-Islam and its destination. *Al-Haqq* also means *An-Noor*, the shining light, and Allah, too, is *An-Noor.* The opposite of light is darkness.

> "Allah is the shining light of *As-Samawat* and Earth." (*An-Noor* 35)

One of the verbs derived from the noun *Al-Haqq* is *huqqa*, which means became evident, firmly obliging, without any doubt, and with absolute certainty. Another such verb is *ahqaqtu*, which means you have provided due and conclusive evidence.

Al-Haqq embodies predominance.

> "To Allah belong East and West. Wherever you turn you meet the face of Allah." (*Al-Baqarat* 115)

Another of those verbs is *ihtaqaqtu*, which means prevailed upon. It embodies exclusivity, for when it belongs to one it may not be shared with another. Another derivative of *Al-Haqq* is *tahqeeq*, which means investigating, searching for evidence of the truth.

Al-Haqq is used in Al-Quran frequently with the following meanings:

(1) Allah, in the singular and with the *al-* prefix.

> "Because Allah is Al-Haqq..." (*Al-hajj* 62)

> "They knew that Allah is evidently Al-Haqq." (*An-Noor* 25)

(2) The cause of creation and all existence and of continuing existence, the source of authority and legitimacy, the point of origin, and fountain of rules.

> "Do you not see that Allah created *As-Samawat* and Earth by Al-Haqq?" (*Ibrahim* 19)

(3) All that Allah created or willed.
(4) Al-Quran and/or Al-Islam.

> "We sent you bearing the good news, and to give notice, of Al-Haqq." (*Al-Baqarat* 119)

> "Allah states Al-Haqq." (*Al-ahzab* 4)

> "He is the one who sent His Messenger bearing guidance and the creed of Al-Haqq." (*Al-Fateh* 28)

> "They dis-believe in the creed of Al-Haqq." (*At-tawbat* 29)

(5) What is holy and pure. *Al-Quds* means pure.

> "He is Allah, the sole divinity, the Holy Potentate." (*Al-Hasher* 23)

(6) What is permanent and does not require authorization, extension, or renewal.
(7) Justice.
(8) Capacity, power, and ability.
(9) What is adjudged.
(10) What must be adjudged.
(11) The true one.
(12) Knowledge.

(13) What is perfectly completed.
(14) What is fully evident.
(15) Death.
(16) Resurrection.
(17) The Day of Judgment.
(18) The Reckoning.
(19) Divine punishment.
(20) Individual rights.

Al-Haqq is permanent, stable, and Allah-sent. Its opposite is a fancy or a whim that always changes.

> "Judge among humans by *Al-Haqq*. And follow not the whims that cause you to stray from the path of Allah." (*Sad* 26)

> "Because those who dis-believe follow falsehood and those who believe follow *Al-Haqq*..." (*Muhammad* 3)

> "Among our creations are an *Ummat* guided by *Al-Haqq* and by *Al-Haqq* maintains justice." (*Al-A'araf* 181)

> "Justice is done among them by *Al-Haqq*." (*Al-zumar* 75)

A derivative of *Al-Haqq* is *haqeeqat*, a noun that means truth. *Al-Haqeeqat* has sanctity which requires protection.

It is very difficult indeed to find in Western languages a single word that provides on its own all the above derivatives and meanings. In languages influenced by Latin, the word *right* is derived from *rectus*, "the erect," and implies that which is straightforward. The word *right* in English and the word *droit* in French both mean direction, right as opposed to left. Many European languages define right as that straightforward thing that does not violate truth and justice. The modern Western legal definition of right is what an individual may enjoy under the protection of law or what the law protects and allows individuals to claim and/or hold and possess. Hence, and in the Western legal sense, a right that is not protected by law or is not enforceable by law is not truly a right.

Al-Haqq further includes claims to life, liberty, dignity, and honor, and the defense thereof. Thus it is certain that *Al-Haqq* has no equivalent in modern European usage.

Al-Haqq is stable, predominant, and supreme. Therefore it is not subject to permission or license by authorities. Hence it is above any and all authority.

Al-Haqq is the source of knowledge, wisdom, honesty, integrity, and justice. It is the heart and mind of the message and Al-Sharia of Al-Islam. The Prophet Muhammad was entrusted by Allah to teach *Al-Haqq*.

Chapter Eleven

THE HUKM OF ALLAH

Al-Quran is the word of Allah. It is the primary source of Al-Sharia. Al-Quran is commonly described as *Az-zikr Al-Hakeem*, which means the spoken words that rule with wisdom and justice. There are groups of *Suwar* and/or *Ayaat* that embody clear and precise rules and are referred to as *muhkamaat* in the plural or *muhkamat* in the singular, an adjective that highlights their unchallengeable clarity and authority. The best translation of *muhkamat* is clear, definitive, and decisive, incapable of adverse interpretation.

> "It is He who sent you down the book of which some *Ayaat* are precise and definitive, and are the mother of the book, and other *Ayaat* that may look alike but are susceptible to various meanings... Allah is the only

one who knows their true meaning."
(*Al Omran* 7)

Establishing the state of peace pursuant to Al-Islam mandates prevention of oppression and corruption and the doing away with oppressors and corruptors. This is where Al-Sharia is applied to repulse oppression, put an end to corruption, and restore the state of peace. This is the *Hukm* of Allah. *Hukm* and its derivatives, directly and through a wide range of interrelated meanings, play a central role in stipulating how Muslims are to govern themselves or are to be governed.

Our best translation of *Hukm* is the wise rule. *Hikmat* is derived from *Hukm*. Its best translation is wisdom. *Hikmat* combines knowledge with justice. The supreme *Hukm* belongs to Allah, who is the supreme *Hakem*. In this sense, *Hukm* means wise and just government, and *Al-Hakem* is the supreme wise and just ruler. Al-Sharia is both the foundation and the pillar of the *Hukm* of Allah.

Al-Sharia is made of *qawa-ed*, the plural of *qaedat*. Each *qaedat* is translated into more detailed *ahkam*, the plural of *hukm*.

The literal meaning of *qaedat* is foundation. Our best translation of *qaedat* in the context of Al-Sharia is general precept or principle. Many *ahkam* are provided in Al-Quran or the *Sunnat*, but most were developed by the learned *fuqaha'*, the plural of *faqeeh*, from the root *fiqh*. The literal meaning of *fiqh* is knowledge, and of *faqeeh* is the learned one. The terms eventually took a more specific meaning. *Al- fiqh* came to mean the science of jurisprudence, of law, and *al-faqeeh* came to mean the jurist, the legal scientist. In practice, *al-hukm* became very closely interrelated with *al-fiqh*.

Upholding Al-Sharia takes place through the application of rules derived from its general principles, mainly through *al-fiqh*. A rule states what things should or should not be, always done in a hypothetical factual event. This must be upheld by officers of government or administrators unless it involves a dispute between several parties. In this event it is applied on a case-by-case basis by a judge.

Hukm also means a decision of an adjudicator, a ruling, a judgment. An adjudicator, whether he is a judge or an arbitrator, is also called *hakem*. The process of settling a conflict is called *muhakamat*, the best translation of which is litigation.

Private parties sue for what is their right. This is called *tahakum*. *Al-hukm*, which means the decision or judgment, sets forth the proper characterization of the dispute, the adjudicator's opinion, and his conclusions. The opinion must be based on the rules. The adjudicator will find for someone who complies with the rules and against another who does not.

Al-Hakem, meaning the ruler or the governor, enforces the *Hukm* of *Al-Hakem*, meaning the judge or adjudicator, if it is not complied with voluntarily.

Al-Ahkam, meaning the rules, come in two categories:

A. Those that state, through commandments, what conduct to follow.
B. Those that state, through injunctions and *Hudood,* what conduct to avoid.

Every other conduct is innocent and free. Certain things fall, however, in the realm of morality and good manners. These are not sanctioned but may be subject to accounting on the Day of Judgment. They fall into two further categories:

A. What is good to do, such as piety, charity, and other virtuous acts. This category is called *mandoub.* Our best translation of *mandoub* is "highly recommended to follow."

B. What is good to avoid, such as bad manners and a foul mouth. This category is called *makrooh.* Our best translation of *makrooh* is "abhorrent and highly recommended to avoid."

Freedom and innocence are the original conditions of human life. Hence to rule is to address the action of whoever commits aggression on those conditions through targeting the life or possessions of individuals or constrains their freedom, thus inflicting damage on them. *Al-Haqq* is upheld by enjoining the commitment of such oppression, reversing it, and/or ordering compensation and punishment against the oppressor.

It is undeniable that all *Al-Ahkam* have their source of legitimacy in the *Hukm* of Allah and take their authority from Allah. This authority makes them obligatory and binding.

> "Resolve every controversial matter among you with reference to Allah and the Messenger." (*An-nisa'* 59)

In applying the rules upon the authority of Allah and His Messenger, there is no room for vanity.

> "Pretension cannot substitute any part of *Al-Haqq*." (*Younus* 36)

Whatever is devoid of authority lacks legitimacy and cannot constitute an enforceable *qaedat*.

> "For which We did not provide authority..." (*Al-hajj* 71)

> "We could not have provided you with authority except by leave of Allah." (*Ibrahim* 12)

Al-Qawa-ed and *Al-Ahkam* are applied in two ways or stages:

A. During a lifetime, by adjudicating conflicts or applying punishments.
B. On the Day of Judgment, through recompensation.

The primary purpose of government is to prevent aggression, oppression, and corruption. This is the main task or duty of a *Hakem*, meaning ruler. It is done through upholding *Al-Ahkam* and vindicating *Al-Haqq* through doing justice.

The modern Arabic word *qanoun* comes from *canon*, which is of Greek origin. It signifies the path or principle. It was also used to mean rule. Its usage came to be limited to Christian churches. Every single church rule is called a *canon*. The plural is *canons*. The Ottoman sultanate borrowed this term in the nineteenth century for use in the reforms it called *Tanzimat*, enacted in a bid to get in line with European modernity. From there it was introduced into Arabic for use in translating the Napoleonic Civil Code. *Qanoun* is now uniformly used in the Arab world to mean positive law in the Western sense.

The *Hukm* of Allah, *Hukm-ul-lah*, differs from rules of law, including constitutional law in Western legal systems, in that such rules are commands legislated under the authority vested in the legislating government which may be amended or repealed. But *Hukm-ul-lah* cannot be amended or repealed. Its core is inalienable right and protects all rights that are by nature inalienable.

While Western codes of law going back as far as the Roman Code of Justinian placed the power of government above the law, *Hukm-ul-lah* ranks higher than the power of government and applies to rulers as well as to commoners. *Al-Hurumat*, plural of *hurmat* which, in our best translation, means sanctity, are prescribed and protected by Allah and may not be compromised. They are inalienable.

> "Whoever upholds *Al-Hurumat* of Allah is favored by his Lord." (*Al-Hajj* 30)

The Prophet Muhammad said, "Every Muslim owes every other Muslim the duty to protect the sanctity of his property, his life and his integrity."

Chapter Twelve

THE ORIGINAL AL-QAWA-ED AL-KULLIAT OF AL-SHARIA

The Purposes of *Al-Haqq* and Al-Sharia

Al-Haqq is steady, firm, and stable. It does not change. It protects the integrity of the universe which includes all the worlds, *Al-Alameen*. It has the same aim on earth, i.e., to protect the integrity of humankind by upholding Al-Sharia and leading humans unto the straight path. This enables the protection of all rights, especially those that are inalienable by their very nature.

The full application of Al-Sharia inhibits aggression and oppression and ensures justice. This is one proof of its legitimacy.

The first step is to rein back human *ahwa'*, which mean fancies or caprices, which may cause or incite aggression and result in material or bodily harm to individuals. *Ahwa'* is the plural of *hawa*.

Al-Ahwa' can be bad and, in such a case, may cause a human to fall into a bottomless pit. There are two main sources of *Al-Ahwa'*: instincts and desires. Instincts are natural and may be good or bad depending on whether they comply with or violate Al-Sharia. Desires are also natural to humans, but they too must be subordinated to Al-Sharia. This is the difference between what is *halal,* or compliant with Al-Sharia, and what is *haram,* or violates Al-Sharia.

> "Do not pursue your caprices but be just." (*An-nisa'* 135)

> "Humans fancy the love of their caprices." (*Al Omran* 14)

> "Many are unknowingly led astray by their caprices." (*Al-An'am* 119)

The Original *Al-Qawa-ed Al-Kulliat* of Al-Sharia

Al-Qawa-ed are the foundations. Al-Sharia consists of *Al-qawa-ed Al-Kulliat,* which translate to general precepts or principles. A single *qaedat* gives rise to a number of detailed *Ahkam* (rules). The purpose of *Al-Ahkam* is to fully implement *Al-Qawa-ed.*

The original *Al-Qawa-ed Al-Kulliat* of Al-Sharia are superior to modern constitutional provisions in that such *Qawa-ed* may not be changed. Governments may not amend or repeal them because they are governed thereby and are subject thereto. Humans are entitled to them by birth and may not alienate them. They are above constitutions, governments, and all powers. What any government may only do is faithfully observe and comply with them. If needed, a government may issue administrative regulations aimed at full observance and protection of *Al-Qawa-ed* and enforcement of *Al-Ahkam* in order to fully uphold *Al-Haqq*.

Al-Ahkam that come down from *Al-Qawa-ed Al-Kulliat* are not to be legislated by government. They arise from *Fiqh* and are the work product of *Al-Fikaha'*.

The original *Al-Qawa-ed Al-Kulliat* protect the *hurumat*, which consist of the following basic and inalienable rights.

The Right to Life and Liberty

Giving life is the most sacred gift of Allah. It arises from creation. To protect it is to glorify the Creator. Life is one of Allah's attributes and is recognized among His Good Names.

> "Allah, who there is no divinity but Him, is the Giver and the Sustainer of life." (*Al-Baqarat* 255)

Human life means little without liberty. Liberty is the antonym of slavery. A human is naturally born free. He enjoys full liberty to the extent he does not commit an offense that requires punishment.

The Right to Resist *Zulm*

A Muslim has the right and duty to resist *zulm* which falls upon or threatens him or others in his ward or under his care or protection. *Zulm* is the antonym of *Haqq*. The gravest form of *zulm* is that which compromises human life. The victim of a murder is *mazloom* because his life was unjustly taken.

> "Those who were oppressed have the right to fight back and Allah is capable of giving them support. Those are the ones who were unjustly driven out of their homes." (*Al-Hajj* 39–40)

> "He who exalts satisfaction for the act of oppression inflicted upon him is beyond reproach." (*Ash-shura* 41)

The Right to Peace and Security

The word *Islam* is derived from *salam*. The linguistic meaning of *Al-Islam* is to enter or join the peace. Peace has many meanings. It is opposite to fighting and war. It is safety from harm. It is innocence. It is forgiveness. It is security. *Al-Jannat* (paradise) is the house of peace. The core of the message of *Al-Islam* is peace. *Al-Islam* preaches, and aims for, peace:

> "All you believers: join the peace without exception." (*Al-Baqarat* 208)

> "Allah calls to the house of peace."
> (*Younus* 25)

Peace secures humans against aggression, oppression, and fear. Security inspires confidence and inhibits treason, just like telling the truth is the opposite of lying. Al-Islam means *sala-mat* (safety) to Muslims. The noun *Muslim* means at peace and in the state of security.

But it is not a necessary precondition to join the peace to be a believer.

> "Do not say to someone who meets you with the greeting of peace: You are not a believer!" (*An-nisa* 94)

The Right to Sanctity of Covenants and Contracts

Al-Islam requires the strict observance of covenants and contracts. It recognizes that private and public interactions between humans are based on a solid series of implicit and explicit contracts. The difference between a contract and a covenant is that a contract is entered into in private transactions such as sale and purchase, rent, and the like. Marriage, too, is a contract. A covenant, however, is made in the public sphere, and when confirmed it becomes a *meethaqq*, a compact. This also applies to international relations.

The first and highest covenant is the one Allah made with humans or humans made with Allah.

> "Fulfill your covenant with Allah if you made one." (*An-nahl* 91)

> "Fulfill your covenant [otherwise] you will be held responsible [for the nonfulfillment]." (*Al-isra'* 34)

The early Muslims made a covenant with the Prophet Muhammad and his successors. This kind of covenant is called *bay-at*. Our best translation of *bay-at* is entering into an obligation to follow and obey the leader. Humans may offer *bay-at* to Allah, to the Prophet Muhammad, and to his successors. The act of *bay-at* is called *mubayat*. It is a covenant entered into between two parties, the people, and their *imam*—that is, leader. The relations between the Prophet Muhammad and *Al-Ansar*, his early supporters from Al-Madina, were founded on two *bay-at* that preceded his *Hijrat* (migration) from Makkah to Al-Madina. They are the first *bay-at* at Aqabat and the second *bay-at* at Aqabat. Al-Ansar offered him their covenant to comply with the message of Al-Islam by upholding the unity of Allah and Al-Sharia and not to commit crimes. The Prophet accepted their offer and made his covenant to side with them in war or in peace.

Covenants between states and other international entities are called treaties.

There are many *Ayaat* that command the fulfillment of contracts.

> "Oh believers, fulfill your contracts." (*Al-ma-edat* 1)

Compacts are above personal loyalties, including the loyalty arising from the unity of creed.

> "If you are called upon by follow Muslims to give support against [their adversaries] you are obliged to come to their support unless it is against people with whom you have a compact." (*Al-anfal* 72)

Compacts and contracts may be entered into even with polytheists, idol-worshippers, and other infidels. Muslims must observe them until the lapse of their respective term.

> "As to those polytheists with whom you entered into a compact and they did not violate it and did not ally themselves against you with anyone, fulfill your obligation towards them until the expiry of its term." (*At-tawbat* 4)

But this is conditional on the other side's scrupulous observance of its contractual obligations. A compact is based on the mutual confidence of the parties.

> "Those who uphold their confidence and their obligation [under their compact]." (*Al-Mou'minoon* 8)

It is said that the Prophet Muhammad was able to subdue a polytheist who assaulted him and tried to kill him. The Prophet then offered him the opportunity to be a Muslim, but the polytheist refused and counteroffered by promising the Prophet never to fight him again or side with a party that intended to fight him. The Prophet accepted and let the polytheist go free.

Covenants and contracts that violate *Hukm-ullah* or the original *Qawa-ed* of Al-Sharia, or lead to the violation thereof, are invalid. The Prophet Muhammad said, "No one is to be obeyed in an act of disobedience to the Creator."

The Right to Sanctity of *Ad-Dyar*

Ad-Dyar is the plural of *dar*, which means house or home. It is where humans live and/or work. Collectively, *Ad-Dyar* means homeland or country. Humans have the right to reside in their *Dyar* and not to be removed from it. Forcing or expelling Muslims out of their *Dyar* is a very grave offense. Al-Islam regards expulsion of Muslims from their *Dyar* the height of oppression and calls for resisting it and, if the expulsion is completed, fighting back until it is reversed. Restoring expelled persons to *Ad-Dyar* is considered a justifiable reason for war.

> "We must fight in the cause of Allah now that we have been expelled from our homes." (*Al-Baqarat* 246)

> "Expel them from where they expelled you." (*Al-Baqarat* 191)

The Right to *Al-Adl*

Al-Adl means justice. It is the opposite of *zulm*. *Al-Adl* is one of the Good Names of Allah. It is the character of anyone who is not influenced by caprice. It is the pillar, foundation, purpose, and *cause d'être* of government and an implicit condition and basis of all human relations. *Al-Adl* mandates upholding *Al-Haqq* and uncovering truth.

> "Allah commands the upholding of justice and charity." (*An-nahl* 90)

> "Do justice, it is closest to abstinence." (*Al-ma-edat* 8)

> "We set up the most accurate of scales for use on the Day of Judgment so that no soul shall be wronged anything and not even the equivalent of the weight of one seed of mustard." (*Al-anbiya'* 47)

> "We have sent our messengers with evidence and sent with them the book and the scale so that humans shall uphold justice." (*Al-hadeed* 25)

> "Weigh with the most accurate and correct of scales and do not deprive people of things that belong to them." (*Al-shuara'* 183)

The most accurate of all scales is called *al-qistas*. This is the scale of justice and the prime condition of *nazahat*, integrity. Integrity is maintained by staying away from everything *makrooh* (abhorrent).

The Right to *Rahmat*
Allah is *Ar-Rahman* and *Ar-Rahim*. The closest interpretation of *rahmat* is mercy.

> "My *rahmat* embraces everything." (*Al-Araf* 165)

> "Do not despair of Allah's *rahmat*." (*Al-zumar* 53)

Rahmat is the gift of Allah, yet every individual has the right to *rahmat*.

The Right to *Jihad*
Al-Jihad means devotion to the upholding and defense of Al-Sharia and one's personal beliefs through best possible efforts. This includes enlisting in the army to fight a just war.

> "Fight further to the path of Allah those who fight you." (*Al-Baqarat* 190)

> "Devote your moneys and yourselves to follow the path set by Allah." (*At-tawbat* 41)

> "Those who believe in Allah and the Day of Judgment need no permission

to be devoted to the path of Allah."
(*At-tawbat* 44)

The Right to Social Welfare and Solidarity

Al-Islam embodies the thought that Allah *yarzuq*—provides nourishment for—his creation. *Ar-Razzaq*, Provider, is one of the Good Names of Allah. The noun is *rizq*.

> "Allah provides nourishment for every creature that moves on Earth." (*Hood* 6)

> "Those whose riches are subject to a definite right by the pauper and the disinherited…" (*Al-ma'arej* 24)

Certain groups are at a disadvantage in receiving sufficient *rizq*. They are the poor, the destitute, and the homeless. They are entitled to relief through *sadaqat*, which means a contribution or donation, made earnestly as a token of one's belief in *Allah*. *Zakat* means purity: a portion of one's money given for the purpose of purifying the rest. It is a regular *sadaqat* made once a year. *Zakat* is applied either directly or through the authorities, or both, to relieve the disadvantaged.

> "The sadaqaat go to the poor, the miserable, the administrators thereof, and those whose hearts are softened, for buying the freedom of slaves and settling penalties ordered

> in favor of injured parties, and [for other purposes] in the path of Allah, and for the homeless." (*At-tawbat* 60)
>
> "Give [what you owe as] the entitlement of your relatives, the disinherited and the homeless." (*Ar-room* 38)

"How can a nation be sanctified if it does not take from its strong to give to its weak?" asked the Prophet Muhammad.

The Right to the Protection of One's *Ardd*

Al-Ardd is the moral component of the personality of a human, his character, and that of his loved ones, which gives value to its physical component and makes him and his loved ones worthy of respect. It involves a mixture of dignity, reputation, and honor. It is that part of the person which is especially hurt by defamation and slander. Every Muslim is entitled to the protection of his *Ardd* from assault. Muslims should uphold the sanctity of *Ardd* of every Muslim just as they are obligated to protect his life and property, said the Prophet Muhammad.

The Right to the Sanctity of the Home

No one may enter someone else's premises without his permission.

> "Oh believers do not enter homes other than your own unless you secure

the permission of the homesteaders and greet them." (*An-noor* 78)

"If you cannot find any one there do not enter until you receive permission and, if you are told to turn back, turn back." (*An-noor* 28)

The Right to *Izzat*

Izzat is an intense sense of the state of invincibility, well-being, and importance. *Al-Azeez* is one of the Good Names of Allah, the possessor of *izzat* and the unassailable, the invincible. *Al-Mou'izz* is another of the Good Names of Allah, who brings about *izzat*. *Izzat* is the opposite of *zillat*, which is the state of being subdued, disgraced, and degraded. Every believer is entitled to *izzat* in equality. This does not, however, imply any superiority among each other or vis-à-vis other groups.

> "*Al-izzat* belongs to Allah, to his Messenger and to the believers." (*Al-munafiqoun* 8)

The Right to *Ismat*

Ismat is the state of being protected and unharmed. It translates into keeping a person's integrity both physically and morally. Privacy is an integral part of it. It is the opposite of slavery and torture.

> "Save yourselves by holding firm to the ropes of Allah." (*Al Omran* 103)

The ropes of Allah mean His covenant. Allah may provide *ismat* on his own. Addressing the Prophet Muhammad:

> "Allah will protect you from humans." (*Al-ma-edat* 67)

It is said that the Prophet Muhammad once sent away his detail of personal guards saying, "Go away, Allah *asamani.*" *Asamani* is a verb which means "gave me *ismat,*" which is His protection.

Ismat is a condition of life and liberty. The *ismat* of a woman is her marriage, because it is the duty of the husband to ensure her protection.

Ismat is the opposite of the state of slavery. Al-Islam did not ban slavery outright but gave Muslims every incentive and inducement to free slaves. Freeing slaves is highly recommended, *mandoub*. Many *Ayaat* call for *tahreeru raqabat,* i.e., "freeing a neck."

The Right to *Al-Karamat*

Al-Karamat is respect and honor. Its best translation is dignity.

The Right to Innocence as a Matter of *Fitrat*

Al- Fitrat means creation. It is what a human is endowed with when created.

> "It is the creation of Allah that fashioned humans, and the creation of Allah is unchangeable." (*Ar-room* 30)

A human is created endowed with *bara-at* (innocence) and *husn an-niyat* (good faith), the ability to distinguish *halal* (what is normally acceptable) from *haram* (what is not normally permissible), and making the right choice of what is *halal*. *Al-fitrat* is always whole.

Al-bara-at is original. This sharply contrasts with the Christian doctrine of original sin. The concept of *al-bara-at* in Al-Islam is far superior to the presumption of innocence in modern Western law. *Al-bara-at* of a human is original and stands firm until it is established that he has incurred liability as a result of a legitimate event, duly proven. There is no question of a presumption. Someone who challenges *al-bara-at* has the burden of proof. The same goes for good faith. It is original, and someone who wishes to challenge it has the burden of proof.

The Right to *As-Sawa'*

As-Sawa' is just equality in benefit, harm, punishment, and reward. All humans are *sawasiat*, that is, equal. *Sawa'* also means straightforward. *Sawyat* means togetherness in equality. Justice must be done with *sawyat*, that is, in equality and without prejudice for or against any of the parties.

> "Say Oh People of the Book: we ask you to join us in a word of justice in equality with us." (*Al Omran* 64)

The Prophet said, "The nations that preceded you perished because when a man of nobility committed theft he was let alone, but when a commoner did it he was punished." He also said, "Humans are equal like the teeth of a comb."

As to gender, the original state preached by Al-Islam is equality. But it is the duty of men to be fair to women and to protect them.

> "Men shall give support to women whenever Allah endowed them with an advantage that women lack." (*An-nisa'* 34)

Such support is mandated by the advantages of the stronger biological constitution and socioeconomic role of a man over the biological construction and the social role of a woman. The two sides of the equation come to a balance in *as-sawa'*. Each man and woman shall be rewarded for the part they play in achieving this balance.

> "Men shall be rewarded for their part and women shall [also] be rewarded for their part." (*An-nisa'* 32)

Differences between spouses must be resolved in arbitration under conditions of *as-sawa'*.

> "If a break-up in their relationship is feared then submit to one arbitrator from his parents and one arbitrator from her parents." (*An-nisa* 35)

The Right to Nondiscrimination

This right is a byproduct of *as-sawa'*. A human is distinguished from other humans according to the extent of his abstinence, *taqwa*.

> "The most abstinent among you is the most favored by Allah." (*Al-hujurat* 13)

The Right to Free Expression and Belief

The freedom of belief is protected. So is the freedom of expression. Converting from one religious belief to another must take place conscientiously and via discussion and free expression of thought. The early struggle of the Prophet Muhammad and his companions in Makkah aimed mainly at ensuring their ability to freely express their belief and give notice of the message of Al-Islam. This was denied them and they became subject to severe oppression. Hence their compulsory migration to Al-Madina.

> "There is no compulsion in creed for the true path is distinctly evident and distinguished from going astray." (*Al-Baqarat* 256)

> "You have your creed and I have mine." (*Al-kaferoon* 6)

> "Al-Haqq came from your Lord. Who wishes to believe in it is free to do so. Who wishes not to believe in it may do so." (*Al-kahf* 29)

The great differences in beliefs between Al-Islam on the one hand and Christianity and Judaism on the other hand, as well as between Christianity and Judaism, are acknowledged by Al-Islam. Al-Islam takes the position that Allah alone will adjudicate those differences on the Day of Judgment.

> "On Judgment Day, Allah will adjudicate between those who believe, the Jews, the Sabians, the Christians, the Magicians and the polytheists." (*Al-hajj* 17)

> "You will adjudicate among your worshippers their differences." (*Al-zumar* 46)

The above does not apply, however, to the renunciation of Al-Islam by Muslims.

The Right to Knowledge

"Read!" It is a commandment and the first word in the first *Ayat* of the first *Surat* in the revelation of Al-Quran. The most significant meaning of this commandment is: learn! Everyone has the duty to educate himself and acquire *al-ilm*, which means knowledge or science. The best translation of *alem* is a learned man, a scientist. Its plural is *ulama*.

> "Say: Oh my Lord, endow me with more knowledge." (*Taha* 114)

Knowledge is one of the attributes of Allah. The Prophet Muhammad said, "Seek knowledge even if in China." It is derived from the verb *arefa*, which means knew. One of its commonly used derivatives is *al-maarouf*. This means a customary good deed. *Al-irfan* is synonymous with *al-ilm*.

Al-Quran is full of praise for the *ulama*, the plural of *alem*, and shows high appreciation for their role in society. It looks at *al-ilm* as the road to Al-Islam.

> "Of all Allah's worshippers, it is the scientists who fear Him most." (*Fater* 28)

> "It is those who are most knowledgeable, and the believers, who believe in what was sent down to you." (*An-nisa'* 168)

A deficiency in *al-ilm* raises the risk of *ddalal*.

> "Humans were led astray due to their lack of knowledge." (*Al-An'am* 144)

The Right to Participate in Public Affairs

Muslims have the right and duty to take part in the affairs of state through:

A. *Shura*. The original linguistic meaning of this word is to seek honey from the hive. The verb is *ashara*, which means gave a sign. *Ashara* came to mean seeking other people's opinion and consent. They would give it in response to a question by making a sign of approval or disapproval. Some offer their *shura* more elaborately. Muslims should make their decisions in *shura* among each other. *Shura* does not mean giving only advice or counsel, but also consent.

> "Their affairs should be conducted by mutual *Shura*." (*Al-shura* 38)

The Prophet said, "My nation will not unite in support of evil." In modern terms, *Shura* can take the form of general elections or referenda.

B. *Al-Bayat.* The contract of *Al-Bayat* is formed by the exchange of offer and acceptance for the purpose of naming *imams*. The first contract of *Al-Bayat* was offered to and accepted by the Prophet Muhammad by *Al-Ansar*, a group of his supporters from Al-Madina. In modern terms, *Al-Bayat* can take the form of approval in general elections of a candidate for office, which also signifies a contract.

> "Those who contract with you are in reality contracting with Allah because the hand of Allah is above their hands." (*Al-fateh* 10)

C. *Al-Jihad.*

The Right to the Sanctity of Private Property

No private property may be taken without its owner's consent except through bankruptcy proceedings to satisfy his debts. Expropriation and eminent domain are not recognized by *Al-Sharia*.

Ownership of gifted property does not change hands until the donor voluntarily delivers possession of the gift. The benefit of contracts must be ensured through free compliance or by compulsion in the enforcement of a judgment.

The Right to Independent Personality

A person is recognized as having full legal personality upon attaining majority. At that time he acquires the ability to obligate himself. Each person is entitled individually and independently to his own financial net worth consisting of assets and liabilities. The rights of a minor are exercised on his behalf by his father, naturally, or another guardian appointed by a judge. The ability to exercise the rights to which an independent person of legal majority is entitled may only be curtailed by a judge for good reasons to protect him or his creditors such as in the event of madness, profligacy, or bankruptcy.

The Right of Women to Equality

Al-Islam ensures this right. A woman is entitled individually and independently to her own independent financial net worth consisting of assets and liabilities. She loses none of her personal assets upon marriage. Her family name does not change. She may buy and sell property and engage in commerce on her own. In early Islamic history, women played prominent roles. Many women who believed in Al-Islam migrated from Makkah on their own initiative, often defying a father or a husband, to join the Prophet Muhammad in Al-Madina. They joined fighting forces to provide vital noncombat duties such as nursing, cooking, and guarding rear lines. It is not the intent of this book to deal in great detail with the subject of women's rights in Al-Islam, but it is appropriate to explore areas where there is some criticism from certain women's rights advocates.

A. Men and women have equal rights in the face of charges of *zena,* which is when a man and a woman have sexual relations without being married. *Zena* also means adultery in the Western sense, when one of the two parties in the relationship is married. Making a charge of adultery without being able to prove it is a very serious offense and the offender is penalized with lashes. If one of the adulterous parties is married, then the penalty is death by stoning. A husband may not charge his wife with adultery because his word is as good as hers. Substantiation of a charge of adultery requires the testimony of four fair witnesses whose testimony is admissible. The witnesses must together state under oath that they witnessed in great clarity the sexual act itself when the man entered the woman. Alternatively, the person who committed the offense of *zena* may confess out of his or her own free will. One confession is not sufficient. He or she must confess four separate times, with time separating one confession from the other. Still the confessions of one party do not make the other party equally guilty of the offense. A husband who surprised his wife while she was engaging in a sexual act with another man has no right to harm either of the two sexual partners. His witness of the act is not sufficient evidence against his wife and her partner. Death by stoning is a severe punishment indeed, but the intent is to dissuade individuals from engaging in sexual relations outside marriage especially when one of them is married, because Al-Islam values very highly the sanctity of marriage, of which absolute fidelity is a condition. The strict rules of evidence that must be observed to convict someone of this crime are nearly impossible to satisfy, which mitigates the obvious severity of the punishment.

B. Polygamy is acceptable, provided that the additional wives enter into the relationship with open eyes. If a second or a third or a fourth wife enters the marriage unaware of the preexisting marriages, she is entitled to an annulment. Polygamy was widely practiced before Al-Islam. Al-Islam reformed it by introducing a limit of four wives. This reform introduced a precondition for polygamy which is justice, that the husband should treat his wives equally. Furthermore, the fundamental precondition for all marriages must be established, which is *al-kafa'at. Al- Kafa'at* means the parties to a marriage must match each other in qualities. Finally, the economic burden of polygamy is carried singularly by the husband, who must support all his wives or they may bring action to dissolve the marriage. Polygamy is rare in the lands of Al-Islam today. What enables polygamy is war and heavy immigration where the balance of women, who do not immigrate or fight and lose their lives, and men, who do, is seriously disturbed. Under such conditions, polygamy seems to be an act of generosity. And a woman who does not wish to be the second, third, or fourth wife out of her own free will can easily choose not to do so.

C. Inequality in inheritance deserves a closer look. Al-Islam introduced a major and historic reform in establishing a detailed and delicate order for an enforceable right to inheritance, and at the same time giving the individual the right to make a will limited to one third of his estate. Within this order, a married woman gets a reserved and inalienable share of her husband's estate of one eighth if she has children by him, or of one fourth if she does not. The father and mother of the deceased, if they survive him, get one sixth each as reserved shares which are equal. The children get the balance and it is divided among them, with a daughter getting half the share of a son. Before this reform, women did not inherit at all. This system of reserved shares protects the wife from being disinherited through a will, which is possible under most modern laws of inheritance. The inequality in shares is compensated by the duty of a future husband to provide for his wife. This duty is not reciprocated, and a rich wife cannot be forced to support a poor husband. The duty to support extends to the father, sons, and brothers of a woman who is in need of support. But she has no reciprocal duty.

D. The privilege of a husband to divorce his wife by his own free will is much criticized. The wife does not have such privilege under Al-Sharia. Islamic marriage, however, is contract-based and every kind of reasonable condition may be written into the contract of marriage, including the delegation of the privilege of divorce to the wife. If this condition is not written into the marriage contract, a wife may always bring action to dissolve the marriage for valid reasons. Marital conflicts are to be resolved in arbitration by two arbitrators, with each of the spouses or their respective parents appointing one arbitrator. A condition of Islamic marriage that counterweighs the privilege to divorce is the *mahr*, which is the agreed monetary consideration, payable upon concluding the marriage, which matures in the event of a divorce. The *mahr* is often hefty and burdensome for the husband. It is calculated to dissuade him from exercising his privilege. By contrast, the trend in modern family law in the West is to make divorce very simple and easy and nearly at will.

E. One of Al-Sharia precepts that is rarely remembered is that a husband has no right to challenge his parenthood of his child by marriage. As long as the spouses are together, every child belongs to both of them. The only exception is through pleading *zena*, which, as we found earlier, is near impossible. The value of genetic evaluation as evidence is not yet recognized.

F. One of the most wrongly referenced *Ayaat* is the one that states that men are *qawamoon* on women. The literal meaning of *qawamoon* is to have the duty to, to care for, and to be fair and just with. It aims to sustain, honor, and protect the woman and exercise a certain authority to lead the women of the family in justice along the straight path. The natural role that a woman plays in a marriage in bearing and rearing children is complemented by the act of *qyamat* by the husband, who has the duty of caring and protecting.

It should be pointed out that the right of wives to be financially independent, to own their own assets separately, and to engage in commerce has, until recently, been restricted in most European codes. Many Western penal codes absolve a spouse from the crime of killing the other spouse when he or she is surprised in the course of a sexual encounter with a third party. Community property was always assumed to arise from marriage, which resulted in a husband getting the immediate benefit of his wife's patrimony. These are all grave violations of the equality of the sexes and never existed under Al-Sharia.

The Right to Marriage and Family

The seriousness of the offense of *zena* and the severity of the punishment in the event that one of the partners to *zena* is married underlines the value vested by Al-Sharia in the institution of marriage. It is the basis of the legitimacy of succession and inheritance and for sustaining the offspring until they grow up and become self-sufficient. Hence getting married is both a right and a duty. Its purpose is fulfilled with the formation of a family consisting of the spouses and their children.

Al-Sharia does not permit marriage between a Muslim and a polytheist. It does allow, however, a man who is Muslim to marry a woman who is Christian or Jewish. It absolutely prohibits the marriage of a Muslim woman to a non-Muslim man, for such a marriage will not give rise to a Muslim family. The reason is that a non-Muslim husband does not yield to *Hukmul-lah* and hence cannot lead the wife along the straight path. Marriage vests the non-Muslim husband with a certain authority over the family arising from the marriage. If a Muslim woman were to marry a non-Muslim man, this would constitute a violation of the command to Muslims not to yield to the authority of non-Muslims. Finally, the children of such marriage may grow up to be strangers to Al-Islam.

The Right to Inheritance

Inheritance is a consequence of family. Al-Sharia rules ensure certain reserved inheritance rights to prescribed categories of close relatives. These reserved rights are inalienable. Al-Sharia further commands that estates of deceased Muslims are settled according to its rules. Most of these rules are set forth in Al-Quran. Al-Sharia also commands that Muslims write a will. Such a will is valid only to the extent of one third of the estate.

Reserved inheritance rights are invalid if applied to a non-Muslim, such as a Christian wife. The rule is that Christians and Jews cannot inherit from Muslims and vice versa. The purpose is to foster the ability of each of these communal groups to maintain its wealth in the community. But rights may be conferred on a non-Muslim by way of will or gift. Hence in the case of a non-Muslim wife, the husband may will her one third of his estate, which puts her in a position superior to that of a Muslim wife.

The Right to Nonretroactivity of Al-Sharia and to Plead Ignorance of the New Rule as an Excuse for Having Violated It

The *qawa-ed* and *ahkam* of Al-Sharia cannot be applied retroactively. They apply only after people are given notice thereof. A human cannot be held accountable for what he is ignorant of. The first duty of the Messenger of Allah was to give notice of the message to all. Someone who is ignorant of Al-Sharia is not held accountable thereunder.

> "With the exception of what already exists..." (*An-nisa'* 22, 23)

> "For the sake of giving you notice..." (*Al-anaam* 19)

This precept is contrary to the modern legal presumption that no one may plead ignorance of the law. The Prophet has the task not only of bringing the good news of the Message of Al-Islam but also to give notice of Al-Sharia so that believers have the knowledge thereof and hence the obligation to comply therewith.

The Right to Satisfaction through Recompensation

Victims of a crime and their relatives have the right to bring charges seeking the application of the punishments prescribed by Al-Sharia to the perpetrator of such crime. This is different from the modern practice of permitting victims to be civil claimants only. Most crimes fall under *Al-Hudood*. The crime of causing bodily injury or of taking a life comes under *qisas*. *Qisas* comes from the root *qasasa*, having the verb *qassa*, which endows it with many linguistic meanings. One meaning is tracking by following evidence until found. Another meaning is to cut hair and nails, which has long been an Arabic metaphor for taking away power. Hence *qisas* means tracing a crime to its perpetrator, which translates in modern terms to prosecution, and giving him a sort of a haircut, which is punishment. The punishment for bodily injuries, including death, is inflicting like injury on the guilty, but nothing more. So if a victim loses one tooth, the punishment is no more than one tooth. The victim or, if dead, his next of kin, may forgive, for or without consideration, the perpetrator, and that will end prosecution and set him free.

> "Those who cross *Al-Hudood* of Allah are oppressors." (*Al-Baqarat* 229)

> "The recompensation of those who fight Allah and His Messenger and spread corruption on Earth..." (*Al-ma-edat* 33)

The Prophet Muhammad stated, "Where there is doubt, *Al-Hudood* shall not apply." This rule certainly applies to *qisas*.

Conclusion

It is abundantly clear that the original general *qawa-ed* of Al-Sharia aim to ensure the safety and integrity of the individual in body, morale, and property, as well as the safety and integrity of the smaller social unit, the family. They further ensure the sanctity of *ad-dyar* and the security of the human society through the protection of the inalienable rights of every individual and his ability to freely and independently exercise his will.

Chapter Thirteen

RULE DEVELOPMENT UNDER AL-QAWA-ED AL-KULLIAT OF AL-SHARIA: ROLE OF AL-FIQH

It is asserted that Al-Sharia is valid and good for all times and places. This statement is true. It is not valid, however, outside what was provided in Al-Quran. According to the predominant opinion expressed in *al-fiqh*, the *Sunnat* of the Prophet Muhammad, which embodies his sayings and conduct in *his capacity as the Messenger of Allah*, is equally authoritative. Together, Al-Quran and *Al-Sunnat* are called the *Sunnat* of Allah and His Prophet.

Mazhab means the belief, opinion, and/or conclusion to adopt and go by. Schools of *fiqh*, known as *mazaheb*, the plural of *mazhab*, emerged to study the general principles and extrapolate specific rules from every time no such rules clearly existed in the *Sunnat* of Allah and His Prophet. Muslims freely follow one or more schools as a matter of personal choice.

Al-Mazaheb ventured both into *al-ibadat* on the one hand and the civil relations among humans, referred to as *mu-amalat*, on the other hand. A relatively large number of schools emerged and had their disciples and followers. Eventually five such major schools remained. They are *Al-Hanafi*, named after the imam *Abu Hanifat*; *Al-Maleki*, named after the imam *Malek*; *Al-Hanbali*, named after the imam *Ibn Hanbal*; *Ash-Shafe'i*, named after the imam *Ash-Shafe'*; and *Al-Jaafari*, named after the imam *Jaafar As-Sadeq*. Each of the imams played the role of the most authoritative *faqih*. The five schools constitute the mainstream of the *fiqh* of Al-Islam. Several other schools of *fiqh* continue to exist and even thrive with millions if not tens of millions of followers who are considered by some mainstreamers as nonmainstream factions and minorities.

The *fuqaha*, plural of *faqih*, took on the function reserved in modern Western states for the legislature. Their opinions were called *fiqh al-ahkam*. Out of those opinions, and those of many of their renowned disciples, came the rules which were to be observed by governments and applied by judges in everyday conflict resolution.

Naturally, these rules, *al-ahkam*, could not violate *Al-Qawa-ed Al-Kulliat* which they were developed to apply to specific sets of factual events. They became, for most intents and purposes, the main working body of Al-Sharia. Nevertheless, it would not be right to assert that they remain valid and good for all times and places.

A judge generally applies the rules of the *mazhab* to which he professes loyalty. Judges, however, were free to pick and choose from more than one *mazhab*. Under the Ottoman sultanate, *Al-Mazhab Al-Hanafi* was decreed to be the official one to be applied in courts. In modern-day Saudi Arabia, *Al-Mazhab Al-Hanbali* is the one. In Iran, it is *Al-Mazhab Al-Jaafari*.

During the nineteenth century *Tanzimat*, or reforms, of the Ottoman sultanate, a committee of jurists was formed to codify *Al-Mazhab Al-Hanafi*, based on a large number of authoritative references. The result of this committee's work is known as *Majallat Al-Ahkam Al-Adlyyat*. This title translates into "The Code of Rules of Justice." It was written in Turkish and translated into Arabic. It is commonly known by the shortened name *Al-Majallat*. The first one hundred articles of *Al-Majallat* were titled *Al-Qawa-ed Al-Fiqhyyat*, which means the general precepts or principles of *al-fiqh*.

Chapter Fourteen

ACCOUNTABILITY: THE PROMISE, THE WARNING, AND THE RECOMPENSATION

Al-Hisab is the promise and warning of Al-Quran to every human. *Al-Hisab* means accounting, which is the process of keeping a record of debits and credits and drawing conclusions therefrom. *Al-Hisab* is concerned with counting the deeds of every human in order to determine the responsibility of the individual for the consequences of his actions during his lifetime and to recompensate him or her accordingly. The Day of Judgment is also the Day of Accounting.

> "The day Allah resurrects them all and presents them with an account of what they did..." (*Al-mujadalat* 6)

The promise of *Al-Hisab* has the primary purpose of dissuading the oppressors, the corruptors, and the criminals from doing what they set out to do in violation of Al-Sharia, and, if their responsibility is determined, to penalize them for their transgression. The process of *Al-Hisab* involves questioning every subject and the finding of evidence for and/or against him in order to ensure that justice is applied.

> "Today there is no oppression. Allah's accounting is fast." (*Ghafer* 17)

> "To Us they come. We do the accounting." (*Al-ghashiat* 25, 26)

> "Allah dislikes corruption." (*Al-Baqarat* 205)

A Muslim is encouraged to practice self-accounting and self-questioning in order to determine his own responsibility.

> "Read your record book. You can, on your own, do the accounting for yourself." (*Al-isra'* 14)

True believers observe Al-Sharia out of *takwa* and conviction. Those who are not true believers or who violate Al-Sharia are to be brought to accounting and questioning.

> "Your task is to give notice. We do the accounting." (*Ar-raad* 40)

> "Allah shall recompensate every soul for what it earned." (*Ibrahim* 51)

> "You shall be accountable to Allah for what you show as well as what you hide."

The *Ayaat* carry the promise of recompensation for good as well as for bad deeds.

> "The punishment of Allah is severe." (*Al-anfal* 133)

Accounting and questioning are performed in accordance with *qist*, which is the most sensitive and accurate of all scales.

> "We set the most accurate of scales for the Day of Judgment so that no soul may suffer injustice." (*Al-anbiya'* 74)

> "He who did a good deed as light as the *mithqal* of a seed of corn shall see it. He who did a bad deed as light as the *mithqal* of a seed of corn shall also see it." (*Az-zalzalat* 7, 8)

> [A *mithqal* is a weight said to be equal to 1/400 of an ounce.]

It results in ascertaining responsibility in justice.

> "There could be no recompensation for charity except charity." (*Ar-Rahman* 60)

Allah promised to reward the abstainers, *al-muttaqeen*, and to punish the violators. He surely keeps his promise.

> "The promise of Allah is assured." (*Al-qisas* 13)

> "Allah's promise cannot fail." (*Ar-room* 6)

> "His is a true promise." (*Mariam* 54)

Judgment and recompensation take place twice: first during the lifetime and second on the Day of Judgment. The recompensation, however, differs in kind. In life the penalty is applied in accordance with the rules of *hudood* and *qisas*. In the ever-after it is committal either to Hell or to eternal life in Paradise.

Chapter Fifteen

CLEMENCY: AL-SAFH THROUGH AL-AFOU, AL-GHIFRAN, AND AT-TAWBAT

Our best translation for *al-safh* is clemency or forgiveness in general. It is the essence of *al-afou*, which means pardon or amnesty; *al-ghifran*, which is forgiveness by Allah; and *al-tawbat*, which is the act of repenting. There is such great virtue in all these forms of clemency that the Good Names of Allah include *Al-Afouw, Al-Ghafoor, Al-Ghaffar,* and *At-Tawab*.

Accounting and questioning followed by establishing responsibility do not necessarily result in recompensation. The books may be closed on the offender through one of the various forms of clemency.

Al-Afou

This means granting a release from punishment. It is a restoration of good standing, which is akin to bringing back good health to a patient. In Arabic good health is *afiat*. It is an act of mercy to an offender whose guilt has already been established.

Unlike pardon, *al-afou* is not a prerogative of government but of the victim who was bodily injured, or, if dead, of his heirs. It could be for a consideration called *dyat*, or for no consideration. *Al-afou* by the victim or his heirs earns the offender the *afou* of Allah as well. If the injury was not intentionally inflicted, *dyat* offered by the offender to the victim or his heirs must be accepted and *al-afou* may not be withheld.

Believers are encouraged to grant their *afou* where possible.

> "If you forgive it is nearly as good as abstinence." (*Al-Baqarat* 237)

> "Let them pardon and forgive." (*An-noor* 22)

Al-Ghifran

This is an act of Allah. It means hiding behind a curtain, effacing, expunging the offenses, and reinstating. In principle, *al-ghifran* takes place on the Day of Judgment in recognition of a good deed or upon acceptable *tawbat* or *shafa-at*. A human may ask Allah for His *ghifran*. The verb is *yastaghfir*.

> "Whoever asks Allah for forgiveness will find Allah to be forgiving and all merciful." (*An-nisa'* 110)

The Prophet Muhammad may exercise *shafa-at*, which means intercession, for believers who are guilty of offenses. Allah may accept *shafa-at* of the Prophet and grant *ghifran*.

> "The Messenger sought forgiveness for them." (*An-nisa'* 64)

No *shafa-at* is admissible for polytheists or whoever doubts the unity of Allah. Belief in Allah and Al-Islam is a precondition that may not be waived.

> "The Prophet and the believers may not seek Allah's forgiveness for polytheists even when they are their relatives." (*At-tawbat* 113)

> "Allah will not forgive polytheism but may forgive anything lesser." (*An-nisa'* 48)

Nevertheless, Allah will grant *ghifran* to anyone He chooses with or without *shafa-at* of the Prophet.

> "Allah is forgiving and all merciful."

At-Tawbat

The best translation for *at-tawbat* is repentance. It is considered to be the shortest avenue to clemency and hence *ghifran*. Asking Allah for *ghifran* may meet His acceptance.

> "Oh you believers: repent to Allah." (*At-tahreem* 8)

> "He accepts repentance by His worshippers." (*Ash-shourah* 25)

An essential condition for *at-tawbat* to be admissible and leading to the desired result is for it to be sincere and inclusive by way of admission of the offenses committed by the repenter.

Al-ghifran and acceptance of *tawbat* are gifts of Allah. They result in the closure of the guilt and the release of punishment.

Section Five

CREED: MEANING THE NATION AND THE STATE

Chapter Sixteen

AL-UMMAT

It is already established that Al-Islam is a creed with multiple meanings. One meaning is belief, faith, and the worship of Allah. Another meaning is *Al-Haqq*, Al-Sharia, sovereign power, and recompensation. *Al-Ummat* came to mean the creed and the sharia, and, at the same time, those who followed them. *Al-ummat* of the Prophet Muhammad consists of the Muslims.

The linguistic root of this word is *amama*, which means *amma*, the best translation of which is the act of journeying to a destination. The term *imam* comes from the same root. He is the leader of those people who are journeying on the straight path. Those constitute an *ummat*. *Al-umm* is the banner followed by the army. Each prophet had his own *ummat*. Under Al-Islam the term *Al-ummat* is synonymous with *sunna-tul-lah warasuluh*. It means the creed and Al-Sharia of Al-Islam and its followers. *Al-ummat* of Al-Islam consists of all the Muslims.

The Islamic *ummat* is not only distinguished by the following of Al-Islam and its prophet and messenger, Muhammad, but, more significantly, with the covenant and compact that bind the Muslims and their submission to Al-Sharia. In modern terms, the Islamic compact is the source of legitimacy of *Al-ummat* and its foundation is Al-Sharia.

The Islamic compact was entered into with Allah by the Muslims who individually accepted the Islamic message as expressed in Al-Quran.

> "Those who uphold the compact of Allah and do not violate the compact…" (*Ar-raad* 20)

> "Did they not join the compact of the Book which provides that they may not say anything of Allah except what is right?" (*Al-araf* 169)

> "We have accepted their compact not to shed their blood." (*Al-Baqarat* 84)

Each Muslim covenants his adherence to Al-Islam by reciting the testimony: "I testify that there is no god but Allah and that Muhammad is the Messenger of Allah." This testimony is also a binding admission and an oath evidencing the witness's commitment to Allah and His messenger and the message sent down by Allah and destined through His messenger Muhammad to all mankind. The task of the Messenger is to report and notify the message entrusted to him by Allah.

> "Their messengers brought them evidence." (*Al-a'raf* 101)

> "He said I am the Messenger of the Lord of the Universe." (*Az-zukhruf* 46)

> "Whoever obeys the Messenger shall have obeyed Allah." (*An-nisa'* 80)

When a Muslim commits himself to the message, he is committed to it in whole, including: (1) creed meaning belief and worship, (2) creed meaning *Al-Haqq*, and (3) Al-Sharia, together with sovereign power and recompensation. The testimony is repeated with every *azan*, call to prayers, and every prayer. *Al-azan* commences with the phrase *Allahu-Akbar*, which means that Allah is greater than anything and everything, including rulers, tyrants, oppressors, and armies. *Allahu-Akbar* reminds one of *al-basmallat*, which is even more widely stated by Muslims and constitutes an admission by Muslims that Allah is *Ar-Rahman Ar-Rahim*. Unbelievers would not say *Allahu-Akbar* or *al-basmallat*.

It is not possible to examine the hearts of humans in order to ascertain how sincere is their belief in Allah and the *ibadat* component of Al-Islam. But when a Muslim commits to Al-Islam, meaning *Al-Haqq* and Al-Sharia, including sovereign power and recompensation, he thereby enters into a compact which makes him part of an *ummat* in the legal and political sense. It is the Islamic *ummat*. It is open to all those who become Muslim. Anyone who becomes a Muslim joins *Al-Ummat* of Al-Islam. The territory on which this *ummat* exists is called *Dar-ul-Islam*, the House of Al-Islam.

In modern times the Arabic term *ummat* is used as the equivalent of nation. The concept of the Islamic *ummat*, however, is radically different from the concept of nation in the West. The origin of the word nation is the Latin *natio*, which means being born in a particular race. The modern definition of nation denotes a body of people possessing a defined territory and organized under one government. An independent nation has sovereign powers that are generally exercised on behalf, and in the name, of its people.

Thus territory is the decisive factor that defines a nation, and all those on the territory become part of it, nationals. In modern times it is possible to grant the nationality of one territory to individuals who move into it from another territory. This is mostly a physical bond based on permanent residence.

The Islamic *Ummat*, however, is constituted on the basis of a legal relationship among individual Muslims. There is no formal grant of nationality. Membership in *Al-Ummat* comes automatically and naturally upon freely joining it, and the new member instantly becomes equal in rights and obligations to all other Muslims, regardless of race or tongue. Simply put, becoming a Muslim is the only condition to becoming a member of the Islamic *Ummat* in *Dar-ul-Islam*.

Chapter Seventeen

THE ISLAMIC STATE

Every time the Islamic *Ummat* and *Dar-ul-Islam* coincide, the potential exists for one or more Islamic states. In modern times, states arise out of the exercise of naked power followed by constitutional conventions or basic laws, which dictate the forms of political organization of the society. If we borrow from the division of constitutional powers generally adopted in modern states, the prototype Islamic state which existed during the first five centuries following the *Hijrat* consisted of the following subdivisions of power:

(1) The executive subdivision was exercised by the imam (regardless of actual titles held) and his subordinates, who had the power and duty to observe and uphold Al-Sharia, including the issuance of ordinances, regulations, and directives for this purpose.

(2) The legislative power was exercised through *fiqh* by one or more *faqih* by devising real-life but hypothetical applications to and solutions under *Al-Qawa-ed Al-Kulliat* of Al-Sharia.

(3) The judiciary power was exercised by the *qadi*, or judge, in the plural *qudat*, appointed by the imam for the purpose of upholding, through adjudication, *Al-Haqq* and justice. *Al-Qudat* applied both Al-Sharia and *fiqh* to actual cases brought before them for adjudication. The *Khalifat* Haroun Ar-Rasheed commenced a policy of appointing a *Qadi Al-Qudat*, or chief justice.

Each of the above subdivisions of power was exercised independently from and in parallel with the other. A fundamental difference exists between the functions of a *qadi* and the functions of a *faqih*. The *fuqaha*, plural of *faqih*, generally resisted and outright refused judge's appointments, even under duress.

In order to more fully understand the Islamic state, one has to deal with the issue of sovereignty in the Western sense. The modern Arabic term for sovereignty is *as-syadat*. Sovereignty in the Western sense means undisputed physical power over a certain territory exercised by a potentate or another form of government. Sovereignty also means the ability to enact new laws and abrogate existing ones. This conflicts with Al-Islam, meaning *Al-Haqq* and Al-Sharia. This is because *Hukm-ul-lah* may not be changed. Furthermore, *Al-Qawa-ed Al-Kulliat* derived from *Al-Haqq* are inalienable. Under Al-Sharia, *Al-Haqq* is always the sovereign, and no individual or group may possess, enjoy, or exercise sovereignty under any pretext.

The *Welayat* of *Al-Imam*

As already discussed, the term *imam* comes from the same root as *ummat* and it means leader unto the straight path. The plural is *ayimmat*. He is the leader, the one who is always up in front. The best translation of *welayat* is authority. This word is derived from the root *walaya*. Whoever has *al-welayat* is called *al-waly*. This term means the person with authority to run things in a certain domain. Each domain of authority is called *welayat*, which is defined as jurisdiction. *Al-walyy* is the ally and protector, the opposite of *adou'*, which means the enemy. The basic *welayat* in an Islamic state are those of *Al-Imam*, meaning the head of state; *al-qadi*; *nazer-ul mazalem*; *nazer al-hisbat*; *al-waly*, meaning the provincial governor; and *ameer-ul-jaish*, meaning the army commander.

The term *imam* is also, and mostly, used for the one who leads the prayers when many Muslims pray together, such as in a mosque. It is also used for other leaders, including those of the infidels.

> "We have made them leaders to guide under our command." (*As-sajdat* 24)

> "Fight the leaders of infidelity." (*At-tawbat* 12)

Al-Imam leads with the benefit of the counsel and consent of the other Muslims as part of the process of *Ash-Shura*.

> "Get their counsel and consent about the affair. If you become certain then rely on Allah." (*Al Omran* 159)

Al-Imam is deemed to be a fiduciary. Being trustworthy is a condition of all *welayat*. The *imamat* of the Islamic state is a duty sanctioned by Al-Sharia. The Prophet Muhammad said, "Of all his creatures, Allah loves most a just *imam*." He also said, "*Al-Imam* must not be obeyed in violation of *Hukm-ul-lah*."

The imam who is head of state is nominated by *ahl al-hall wal-akd* and confirmed by the rest of the Muslims through *al-baya*. *Ahl al-hall wal-akd*, also called *ahl-ul-ikhtiar*, are a group of Muslims in high moral authority who are generally recognized as such by Muslims at large. They are also a group nominated by the incumbent *imam* to perform this function upon his death, as the *Khalifat* Omar Ibn Al-Khattab did.

Al-Mawardy, who lived and wrote in the fifth century of *Al-Hijrat* and was an acknowledged authority on his epoch, highlighted three conditions for membership in *ahl-ul-ikhtiar*—justice, knowledge, and wisdom; and seven conditions for the candidate, which are justice, knowledge, good senses, good bodily parts, good judgment, bravery, and good ancestry.

Al-bayat gives rise to an *imamat* contract between Muslims and their imam. This contract is subject to the conditions of validity and dissolution of all contracts. If *Al-Imam* becomes *fasiq*, that is, corrupted, the *imamat* contract becomes null and void.

Under this contract, Muslims obligate themselves to support and obey *Al-Imam* but always subject to Al-Sharia. In return *Al-Imam* undertakes to protect and uphold the rights of the *ummat*. These rights were enumerated by Al-Mawardy as follows:

(1) Upholding the creed.
(2) Enforcement of judgments.
(3) Maintaining public safety.
(4) Protecting the borders.
(5) Fortifying ports.
(6) Al-Jihad.
(7) Collection of taxes and Zakat.
(8) Determining the entitlements from the treasury to individuals in need.
(9) Employing qualified and trusted people to run the affairs of state.
(10) Administering all policies and matters to advance the interests of the *ummat* and not rely wholly on delegation of authority.

The *Welayat* of the Judge, Fair Trial

Everyone has the right to bring action before the judge so that the judge will rule whereon in a fair trial. Toward this objective, detailed rules of adversarial hearings and evidence were laid down. No one may be judged without being heard and given the opportunity to state his defense and introduce his evidence. The Prophet Muhammad instructed a judge: If you have before you two adversaries, do not rule in favor of one of them before hearing the other that is the defense put forward by the other. The burden of proof is on the plaintiff. Suspicion is not admitted. Innocence is the original state of affairs until guilt or liability is established through acceptable evidence.

> "A suspicion never takes the place of *Al-Haqq*." (*Younus* 3)

> "Some suspicions are evil." (*Al-hujurat* 12)

Responsibility is individual. No one may be made responsible for any part of someone else's actions. Everyone is only recompensated for his own deeds.

> "No burden carrier may carry the burden of another carrier." (*Fatir* 18)

> "Say my deed belongs to me and your deed belongs to you. You are innocent of what I do and I am innocent of what you do." (*Younus* 41)

> "Allah does not compel any soul to do things beyond its ability. Each [soul] is credited with what [good] it earned and charged with what [evil] it is responsible for." (*Al-Baqarat* 286)

When witnesses are heard by way of evidence, each witness must be of high personal integrity, known to be fair and just, and must have no conflict of interest. Such qualifications of a witness must be established before he is heard.

> "Let the just among you testify." (*At-talaq* 2)

> "When you make a statement be just." (*Al-An'am* 158)

The Prophet Muhammad said, "Let the just one testify." These conditions for a witness to qualify serve to provide protection against false testimony.

> "Those [worshippers of Allah] do not give false testimony." (*Al-Firqan* 72)

Most cases require as evidence the testimony of two just and fair witnesses. When *zena* is alleged, the testimony of four such witnesses is obligatory, and they should all testify that they witnessed every detail of the sexual act, including the physical entry of one of the partners into the other. If such evidence fails to materialize, the complainant is held guilty of defamation and is punished. If the *zena* allegation is made by a husband against his wife, her word is more conclusive than his and would absolve her.

> "As to those who accuse their spouses [of adultery] without bringing witnesses, each of them may testify four

> times under oath to Allah that he told the truth, and a fifth time summoning upon himself the curse of Allah if he were a liar. [The wife] may be absolved of guilt if she testifies four times under oath to Allah that he is a liar, and a fifth time that wrath of Allah be upon her if he were truthful."

In the letter of judicial appointment by the Khalifat Omar Ibn Al-Khattab to Abi Moussa Al-Ashari, Omar gave the instructions which became a model of basic rules of procedure for all judges to come. Among those is the rule that a judge may retract his ruling and reverse himself if he becomes convinced that he grossly erred in judgment:

> "You shall not be precluded by a judgment you gave yesterday, but later made a review that guided you to a wiser conclusion, from reversing [such judgment] and reverting to *Al-Haqq*. For taking refuge in *Al-Haqq* is better than continuing to support an error."

Like a witness, a judge must be fair and just and without any conflict of interest. In a court of adjudication, the adversaries appear before the judge on equal standing without any differentiation. One of the most important conditions of justice is the equality of the adversaries before a judge. Al-Quran is full of phrases commanding that the most sensitive of balances, *alqist* or *al-qistas*, are to be used in weighing conflicting claims.

> "When you adjudicate among them rule by the most sensitive balance." (*Al-maedat* 42)

> "The ruling among them was made by the most sensitive balance." (*Younus* 54)

Al-Qist is also one of the Good Names of Allah and means the Just.

Adversaries may reconcile their differences and enter into a peace agreement, *solh*. Such agreements are admissible provided that they do not violate Al-Sharia such as by admitting what is *haram* or denying what is *halal*.

Welayat Al-Mazalem

Al-Mazalem means acts characterized with *zulm*, oppression. The need arose during the *Amawi* era for a channel to the grievances arising from *zulm* in two main areas:

A. Rolling back the influence of the powerful and upholding the rights of the disadvantaged where the power of the executive branch of government is not adequately offset by the power of the judiciary.

B. Where judgments require enforcement due to lack of voluntary compliance.

According to Al-Mawardy, *Welayat Al-Mazalem* included jurisdiction over:

(1) Aggression and other tyrannical exercise of power by a *Waly* against the people. This condition was described in a speech by Khalifat Omar Ben Abdel Aziz as follows: Certain *welat* (plural of *waly*) obstructed *Al-Haqq* until it was purchased from them, and upheld falsehood until they were paid a ransom to let go of it.

(2) Excesses in tax assessing or tax collecting.

(3) Ensuring the integrity of public records through ensuring the honesty of clerks such as in correctly recording the state revenues collected.

(4) Ensuring that entitlements of the persons who earn their living from the public treasury, such as government employees, soldiers, and welfare beneficiaries, are paid in a timely fashion.

(5) Reinstating usurped ownership rights to property seized unlawfully.

(6) Corruption in the administration of awqaf. Awqaf is the plural of wakf, which is real property placed in trust for private or public purposes.

(7) Enforcement of judgments, particularly against influential and powerful persons.

(8) Intervening in matters of *hisbat* where the *Waly* is unable to perform his duties.

(9) Protection of religious practices and festivities.
(10) Adjudicating over persons involved in riots.

The difference between the *Welayat Al-Mazalem* and *Welayat* of the judiciary is that the former does not use an adversarial process and may invoke its jurisdiction and powers without being petitioned, including the gathering of evidence and the summoning of witnesses. The *Waly* is appointed from among people with strong and independent personality. Al-Khalifat often exercised in person the powers and functions of this *welayat*.

It is very interesting that, in modern times, many Western states adopted *Welayat Al-Mazalem* in the form of the institution of the *ombudsman*. This came about originally in Sweden in the year 1809. Other Scandinavian countries followed suit in the 1950s. It has very recently become fashionable as well for private corporate entities to adopt a variation of this system.

Welayat Al-Hisbat

Al-Hisbat is the equitable power to prevent and/or to put an end to *al-munkar*, which means the abhorrent, and enforce *al-maarouf*, which means the customary good. *Waly Al-Hisbat* is also called *Al-Muhtaseb*. His jurisdiction involves the injunction and removal of things considered *munkar* and the protection of *al-maarouf.* He acts of his own initiative.

Al-Mawardy explains that *Al-Hisbat* is a bridge between the jurisdiction of the judiciary and that of *Al-Mazalem*. *Al-Muhtaseb* does not use an adversarial process, nor does he examine the substance of any situation. He is exclusively concerned with what is *zaher*, which means apparent and manifest. If the *zaher* is challenged, the case is referred to the judge for adjudication.

Enforcement of *al-maarouf* involves the apparent and manifest rights and is of two types: public and private. *Al-Muhtaseb* acts in events such as the flooding caused by municipal water or the collapse of a public building or facility. He orders corrective measures such as repairs or reconstruction. He collects *Zakat* when it is not paid voluntarily. He reprimands someone who drinks alcohol in public. He protects consumers by preventing fraud, such as in scales or the quality of goods. He oversees the practice and workings of artisans, as well as practitioners in various vocations, to ensure their honesty and the quality of their products. He makes sure that ships are not overloaded and are not in danger of sinking. He maintains the integrity of streets and roads. In the private realm he acts against someone who transgresses on the property of his neighbor, such as by building on it and orders the construction demolished. He makes sure that a new building does not command a view of the interior of neighboring buildings.

Al-Muhtaseb keeps an eye on the sound performance of the *welat* of other *welayat*, including the judiciary. Al-Mawardy relates that *Al-Muhtaseb* of Baghdad passed by the court of *Qadi Al-Qudat* and discovered that the *Qadi* had not yet arrived to commence the hearings. He called his clerk and asked him to alert the *Qadi* to the fact that a large number of litigants were waiting for him and that if he were unable to come to work for a valid reason he should announce it.

In modern terms the powers of *Al-Muhtaseb* combine the jurisdictions of the inspector general, the prosecutor's office, the judge of summary jurisdiction, the sheriff's office, and more.

Az-Zakat

Az-Zakat is one of the accepted pillars of Al-Islam. The word is derived from *zaka'*, which means development and fruiting. *Zakyi* means delightfully agreeable to one of the bodily senses such as smell or taste. *Zakat* is a superlative of *zakyi*. *Zakat* means purity: a portion of one's money given for the purpose of purifying the rest, and made once a year. It is applied either directly or through the authorities, or both, to relieve the disadvantaged. It is used in Al-Quran to mean purity and blessing.

Az-Zakat is taken from physical and manifest movable property such as currency, merchandise in trade, animal or agricultural products, cattle, and/or precious metals, and the products of mining, which have been in the possession of their owners for over one full year. In Muslim Andalusia it was levied on large holdings of land for the purpose of redistribution. *Zakat* is akin to an offering that purifies the remainder of the property.

"Carry out prayers, pay *Az-Zakat*." (*Al-Baqarat* 43)

"Take out of their wealth sadaqat to purify and cleanse it." (*At-tawbat* 103)

Zakat is a type of *sadaqat*. *Sadaqat* means a charitable contribution, a donation, made earnestly as a token of one's belief in *Allah*. The difference is that simple *sadaqat* is voluntary, while *Zakat* is obligatory and is mostly collected by the state to be applied to welfare.

Hence *Zakat* is an exception to the sanctity of private property and resembles taxation. The Prophet Muhammad said there is no public right in property except *Zakat*. *Zakat* is a levy on non-fixed capital assets and not on income. The capital asset it is levied on is mostly lazy and sits dormant for a full year. It obviously targets the advantaged, which are the rich, much more than the disadvantaged. The property subject to *Zakat* should exceed a certain amount that is exempt. For example, silver is exempt for the amount under 8,400 *mithqal*, an old measure said to be equal to twenty-one ounces. Thirty cows are exempted, and so are forty sheep or goats.

Some interpret Al-Quran to arrive at a rate of *Zakat* of 10 percent. Historically several rates were also used according to the type of property and other conditions. But the prevalent rate of *Zakat* is 2.5 percent.

The beneficiaries from all *sadaqaat*, including *Zakat*, fall into certain categories. First come *al-*

faqeer, the destitute, followed by *al-miskeen*, the poor. Then the welfare workers are paid. The balance goes to every other category of charity such as liberating slaves, helping destitute travelers, and paying fines on behalf of convicts who have no means to make the payment. An old category of *mouallafatu quloubuhum*, which literally means "those whose hearts are softened," constituted a subsidy to certain groups of troublemaking Bedouins for purposes of state, and was abolished under Al-Khalifat Omar Ibn Al-Khattab. The original authority designating the beneficiaries of *Zakat* is in *Ayat* 60 of *Surat At-Tawbat*:

> "The *sadaqaat* go to the destitute, the poor, the administrators thereof, and those whose hearts are softened, for buying the freedom of slaves and settling penalties ordered in favor of injured parties, and [for other purposes] in the path of Allah, and for the homeless." (*At-tawbat* 60)

Section Six

THE RELATIONSHIP OF MUSLIMS TO NON-MUSLIMS IN DAR AL-ISLAM

Chapter Eighteen

THE RELATIONSHIP WITH APOSTATES

Defection from Al-Islam by openly renouncing the testimony or denying the message is called *riddat*, which means going back. The defector is called *murtad* because his *riddat* returns him to the state of *shurk* or infidelity and, ipso facto, makes him an adversary. The closest translation of *murtad* is apostate. *Ar-riddat*, apostasy, is of the magnitude of high treason. Soon after the Prophet Muhammad passed away, some Arabs were involved in *riddat* together with insurgency. This led to what is known as the wars of *riddat*. *Al- riddat* was swiftly put down under the first *Khalifat* Abu Bakr As-Seddeeq.

The American Civil War is in a way similar to the war of *riddat*. It erupted because certain states attempted to withdraw from the union and form a new confederation. Many similar wars have taken place throughout history. Defection in the form of an insurrection often takes the color of high treason in the West, with death as the penalty. Passing state secrets is one of the many kinds of such defection, as is bearing arms with the enemy.

One of the aspects of the wars of *riddat* that is also disturbing is that it is no offense under Al-Sharia when a Muslim joins Al-Islam without harboring true belief in his heart. We have already covered this state of affairs where Al-Islam for certain individuals is merely political, including submission to Al-Sharia, complete with commandments and recompensation. But someone who openly renounces his allegiance to Al-Islam commits an act of aggression on *Al-Ummat* which he had been part of.

Under Al-Sharia, the defector forfeits, upon his *riddat*, all his rights as a Muslim, including his marriage and the right of residence in Dar Al-Islam. Furthermore, he cannot be admitted as a non-Muslim to *ahd-ul-zimmat*.

A non-Muslim who never became a Muslim, however, has no obligation to *Al-Ummat* and vice versa. If a resident of Dar Al-Islam, his status is subject to *ahd-ul-zimmat*.

Chapter Nineteen

THE RELATIONSHIP WITH AHL-UL-ZIMMAT

*Z**immat* means loyalty and devotedness. It is the state of refraining from violating what is sacred and is under Allah's protection, *al-hurumat*, such as covenants and peace. *Al-zimmat* is not individual but collective to all Muslims. *Ahl-uz-zimmat* are the people of *zimmat*.

A *zimmat* covenant, *ahd-ul-zimmat*, commits all Muslims to protect the other parties to the covenant who are not Muslim and ensure their enjoyment of all the rights and guarantees provided under the covenant. Such covenant was entered into with Christians and Jews, through their tribal or religious leaders.

A beneficiary of such covenant is called *zimmi*, or, alternatively, *mu-a-hed*, which means party to a treaty. *Al-mu-a-hed* becomes part of Allah's *hurumat*.

Ahd-ul-zimmat is made for an indefinite duration and continues in full force and effect, unless violated. The violation will affect the individual violator and not the group.

This relationship resulted in the wide participation of non-Muslims in the acquisition and development of the culture and civilization of Al-Islam and everyday life in Dar Al-Islam, which came to a climax in Muslim Spain. It is still so throughout Muslim lands.

Under this covenant, non-Muslims keep their own religious beliefs and the freedom of praying in their own houses of worship. With very few exceptions, the thousands of Christian and Jewish houses of worship that exist today in Islamic lands were built under Al-Islam.

Al-mu-a-hed, however, is, from a civil point of view, subject to Al-Sharia, complete with commandments and recompensation, but with three special provisos:

A. *Al-mu-a-hed* is subject to his group's own personal statutes.
B. *Al-mu-a-hed* has no duty to serve in the military, but he has the option to do so.
C. *Al-mu-a-hed* does not pay *Zakat* but is subject to a head tax called *jiziat* which is commensurate with his income. The *jiziat* levied on a farmer or a laborer is insignificant.

Other than the above *Al-mu-a-hed* falls into the *hurumat* of Allah and enjoys all the freedoms, rights, and safeguards of a Muslim. Should he violate the covenant, he is then treated just like a *murtad*.

With the vast expansion of Dar Al-Islam, much of its indigenous population became Muslim but others did not make this choice and preferred to benefit from *ahd-ul-zimmat*. As a result, scores of non-Muslim denominations survived and flourished in Dar Al-Islam, with their houses of worship, monasteries, clergy, and autonomous councils administrating their religious affairs and family law.

This pluralism emanated from a basic precept of Al-Islam recognizing all preceding religions based on a holy book, and revering all the prophets of Christianity and Judaism and recognizing them as prophets of Al-Islam.

Muslim Spain and *Al-Mashreq* were among the lands in which *ahl-uz-zimmat* flourished most. Spain witnessed the greatest transfer of culture in history from Dar Al-Islam to Europe. Unfortunately, the fall of the Islamic state there was accompanied with the abrogation of *ahd-ul-zimmat* and the ethnic cleansing from Spain of all non-Catholics.

When Egypt became part of Dar Al-Islam, the Coptic patriarch was in jail suffering from Byzantine religious persecution. Muslim authorities released the patriarch and had him reinstated. The Coptic communities of Egypt continue to bloom to this very day, with their people, houses of worship, festivities, and autonomous councils administering all those affairs.

When the heart of *Al-Mashreq*, Syria, including modern-day Lebanon, better known as *Belad Ash-Sham*, became part of Dar Al-Islam, the Christian denominations, which were persecuted under the Roman-Byzantine administration, were liberated. The major cities were opened to the Muslims after the leaders of each city entered into a written *ahd-ul-zimmat*. It is reported that all public offices that were staffed by the *Zimmi* population were kept intact.

The European Crusades, instigated by the Catholic Church leadership, were launched under the slogan of retaking Jerusalem from the Muslims by force of arms and reestablishment of Christian military hegemony in the region around the Holy City. Whenever the Crusaders took a Muslim town, they massacred its population to the last man, woman, and child and brought in European settlers to take their place. The Crusaders did their best to incite local Christians to break their covenant with Muslims.

A case in point is the massacre of the population of Jerusalem, Muslim and non-Muslim. Tens of thousands of Jerusalem Muslims took refuge in the sanctuary of Al-Aqsa Mosque and the Dome of the Rock. It was during the Friday prayers that European soldiers attacked and killed them all. Less than one century later, Muslims retook Jerusalem under the leadership of Sultan Salah-ud-dine Al-Ayoubi, simply known to Europe as Saladin. His sister had been murdered by Crusaders who intercepted a convoy of pilgrims on their way from Egypt to Mecca, together with all other pilgrims in the convoy. After taking Jerusalem, the European Catholic population was allowed to leave the city safely, led by their clergy, who took their treasures with them. The sultan took retribution only on the Crusade commander who murdered his sister.

Upon the final defeat of the Crusaders, life in the Christian communities of Dar Al-Islam resumed its normal and peaceful pace. The same applied to the Jewish communities, which had borne the wrath of the Crusaders on equal footing with Muslims. Today there are thousands of Christian churches in Muslim lands, mostly built under Islamic protection. Their bells ring freely and the faithful attend them for prayer without fear.

It is very significant that Muslims in all Islamic countries were and continue to be very conscious of their role and obligations towards *Ahl-uz-zimma*, and the rights of *Ahl-uz-zimmat*, under the *zimmat* covenant. Some of their thinkers in the Levant had promoted the idea of Arab nationalism as a replacement of the *zimmat* covenant in bringing together Muslims and non-Muslims. They did not fully realize, however, that Al-Sharia protected everyone in Dar Al-Islam equally.

Chapter Twenty

THE RELATIONSHIP WITH AL-KUFFAR

Al-Kuffar, plural of *kafer*, are the disbelievers. Not only do they not believe in Al-Islam, they reject it openly and actively. This condition is called *kufr*. Many *Kuffar* abuse Al-Islam and Muslims verbally or physically, some within Dar Al-Islam but mostly out of it.

> "If you dis-believe, Allah has no need for you. He is not content that any of His worshippers dis-believe." (*Az-zumar* 7)

Al-Kuffar are not necessarily Christians and Jews, but they may be.

> "The dis-believers from among the People of the Book and polytheists were not persuaded until they received good evidence, a messenger of Allah reading holy scriptures." (*Al-bayinat* 1, 2)

> "Those dis-believers from among the People of the Book and the polytheists belong in the fire of hell forever." (*Al-bayinat* 6)

Al-Kufr was actively displayed by the idol-worshippers and some of the People of the Book after, and in spite of, the revelation of Al-Quran and the evidence presented therein. This is taken seriously in Al-Islam, and does not contradict the position it took on the beliefs of the People of the Book. The Prophet said, "Do not say you believe or dis-believe what you hear from the People of the Book [about their religion]. Just say we believe in Allah and his Messenger. Hence if what you are told is right, you do not deny it, and if it is false you do not belie it."

A *kafer* or even a *mushrek* who does not actively reject Al-Islam or attack it or abuse Muslims is another story. We are told that the Prophet Muhammad was able to subdue a *mushrek* who attempted to kill him. The Prophet invited him to become a Muslim. The *mushrek* refused but pledged not to fight the Prophet or to join any group that sought to fight him. The Prophet released him and let him go free.

Chapter Twenty-One

THE RULE OF AL-SHARIA SUSPENDED IN LEBANON: A CASE STUDY

It would not be an exaggeration to recognize that the entire modern political history of the Republic of Lebanon revolves around the open issue of maintaining Maronite Christian political hegemony, or at least parity, vis-à-vis Lebanon's Muslim population. This issue has produced the strongest impediment to the emergence of a true Lebanese national identity and citizenship, with full respect for the rule of law.

Role of the Maronite Church

The central role of the Maronite Church, before and after Lebanon achieved statehood, and its political leadership of a distinctly Christian political establishment, cannot be ignored. The rise of the power of this church must be seen in its historical perspective. This church started as independent and outside the mainstream long before reaching full affiliation with the Roman Catholic Church.

The Roman Catholic Church had little or no presence in the Middle East until the Crusades. The first crusade commenced in 1096 upon the orders of Pope Urban II at the Council of Clermont, which he had convened in November 1095. It took two centuries of Crusades for the Crusaders to be finally defeated. Within that period, the Roman Catholic Church established increasingly strong links with various independent Middle Eastern churches including the Maronite Church, leading, by the eighteenth century, to the full incorporation of the Maronite Church as an autonomous unit of the Roman Catholic Church, and, by the twentieth century, the patriarch of the Maronite Church's becoming a cardinal of the Roman Catholic Church.

The Crusades

French Crusaders established a special relationship with the Maronite community, and many Maronites fought along their side. It is said that a delegation of twenty-five thousand Maronites went to Acre, Palestine, to welcome the landing of the French Crusader King Louis IX in 1250. Later that year, Louis IX sent the Maronite Church a letter of commitment in which he stated, "We are persuaded that this nation that we found established under the name of St. Maroon is part of the French Nation. For its friendship to the French resembles the friendship among themselves." [5]

Louis IX promised protection to the Maronite patriarch and his parish similar to that accorded to the French themselves. The French king was declared a saint by the Catholic Church after he led three unsuccessful crusading campaigns into Egypt, Palestine, and Tunisia, in that order, with the last of his Crusades ending with his death.

The crusades came to a final end with the defeat of the Crusaders in Tripoli in 1289, followed by their defeat in Acre in 1291. In the ensuing battles in the hills around Tripoli with certain Maronite forces formerly allied with the Crusaders, the Maronite patriarch Antoine himself was killed. It was unprecedented for a leader of the Christian clergy to be killed by Muslim soldiers.

Sykes-Picot

The Republic of Lebanon stands on territories that were for several centuries part of the Ottoman sultanate, and before that, from the seventh century CE, of many Islamic kingdoms, commencing with the three historic caliphates of the Rashideen, the Umaweyeen, and the Abbasyeen. The French claimed the Ottoman territories of Syria, including those that were to become the State of Greater Lebanon, pursuant to a secret agreement they had concluded with Britain on May 16, 1916. Called the Sykes-Picot Agreement, it defined the way the two countries wished to distribute among themselves the Ottoman territories of the Middle East after the expected defeat of the Ottomans in World War I. In short, the agreement allotted Iraq and Palestine to the British, and Syria and Lebanon to the French. The Sykes-Picot Agreement was in sharp conflict with the pact that the British had with the Arab Kingdom of Hejaz led by Prince Faisal, a kingdom that fielded military forces that fought the Ottomans on the British side. So Prince (later King) Faisal entered Damascus and established his government there on the faith of the Arab-British Agreement. He accepted the declaration of loyalty from Beirut and Baabda, the seat of the autonomous Sunjuk of Mount Lebanon, and his flags were raised in both cities.

The Sykes-Picot Agreement was revealed by Lenin following the Bolshevik Revolution, and it became a matter of time before the true intentions of the allies, France and Britain, were tested. When Faisal refused to relinquish Damascus peacefully, the French army, led by General Henry Gourau, defeated the Arab army at Maysaloun on the outskirts of Damascus on July 24, 1920, and entered the city triumphantly the following day. The French general promptly visited the tomb of Saladin and announced to the dead Muslim hero that his people, known to Saladin's contemporaries as "the Franks," were indeed back. After securing Damascus, Gourau returned to Beirut where, on August 31, 1920, he issued a decree declaring the annexation of the occupied *Welayat* of Beirut, including most of South Lebanon and part of the

Biqaa; the *Welayat* of Tripoli, including Denniah and Akkar; and parts of the *Welayat* of Damascus, being the Qadha of Biqaa, the Qadha of Baalbek, the Qadha of Hasbaya, and the Qadha of Rashaya, to Mount Lebanon. The following day, September 1, 1920, Gourau issued another decree ordering the birth of "Greater Lebanon" from all those territories. On September 29, 1923, France received a League of Nations mandate over Syria and Greater Lebanon. In 1926, Greater Lebanon was renamed the "Republic of Lebanon" under the constitution of May 23, 1926.

Fall of the Ottoman Empire

The peoples of the Middle East were deeply wounded with the resounding defeat of the Ottoman army at the hands of the British and the routing of King Faysal's Arab forces at the hands of the French, and were further profoundly insulted by the treachery of the British. General Henry Gourau was a reincarnation of sorts of Louis IX. Saladin, Kurdish by ancestry, was a native of Baalbek and an all-time Muslim/Arab hero. But now he was being derided in his grave with the remarks of the arrogant French general who believed that he was in Beirut and Damascus to fulfill the mission of the Crusaders. From then on the destiny of the Republic of Lebanon was heavily influenced by the conflict between Western influence, led successively by France, Britain, and the United States, and Lebanese aspirations for real independence in harmony with Lebanon's natural Arab/Islamic environment.

Gourau Declares "Greater Lebanon"

When General Gourau was making his announcement about Greater Lebanon, he had the Maronite patriarch Elias Hoayek to his right. To Gourau's left was the mufti of Beirut, Mustafa Naja, but the mufti's presence was little more than show. Patriarch Hoayek had played an active role in the preparation for that historic moment. He had been to Paris several times at the head of delegations of Maronite bishops advocating for the formation of Greater Lebanon. Many modern-day Lebanese credit Hoayek with giving birth to what became the Republic of Lebanon. But the role of the Maronite Church in this event was not confined to the event itself.

The Maronite Church and the Republic of Lebanon

Since September 1, 1920, the leadership of the Maronite Church has, both overtly and covertly, played a major role in Lebanese politics. Under the French mandatory power, the political institutions of the country were dominated by Maronite politicians who were often former employees of the office of the French High Commissioner. But no Maronite would serve in any office if vetoed by the church. The patriarch continues to this day to exercise the role of final arbiter among Christian politicians and to exercise an informal yet decisive veto power in Lebanese politics as a whole.

In 1920, it was generally assumed by the Maronite Church and the French military command in Beirut that the ratio of Christians to Muslims among the population of Lebanon was fifty-five to forty-five. The population census of 1932, however, though incomprehensive, failed to conclusively validate this ratio, and it was never updated or repeated. The fifty-five–forty-five ratio was not given any political significance until the year 1943, when Lebanon declared itself independent despite French objections, which were swiftly overridden by the superior British military presence under General Spears. But it the population ratio was slightly modified to six to five, which was reflected in the subsequent general elections laws. In 1991, that ratio was changed to fifty–fifty.

Demographic Changes

Hand in hand with this political amendment (which was part of Taef), the office of the president continued to be reserved to the Maronites but was stripped of much of its powers. As no population census was made after 1932, population figures were estimated. Intelligent population estimates today put that ratio at very close to twenty–eighty and receding fast, as the Muslim Lebanese population is much younger than the Christian Lebanese population and its rate of emigration is substantially lower.

The National Pact

The moment of transition to independence away from France and a partial return to the Arab/Islamic neighborhood marked a new political fiction conveniently called the "National Pact," consisting of a reciprocal concession that Lebanon would have an Arabic face but no more, and that the destiny of Lebanon would be linked neither to France nor to the Arab world, meaning that Lebanon would seek neither political unity with the Arab countries nor political alliance with France and the West. This fiction lasted till February 22, 1958, when the constitutional merger of Syria and Egypt was declared under the leadership of Egyptian President Gamal Abdel Nasser. Lebanon was already suffering from bad political turmoil marked by divisive general elections under the shadow of a definite political tilt by the Lebanese government in favor of the West. These were the days of the Eisenhower Doctrine and the Baghdad Military Pact, which came on the heel of the tripartite invasion of Egypt by the combined Israeli-British-French military forces, ending in a massive political victory for Nasser, elevating him to a modern-day Saladin. The situation in Lebanon quickly escalated into a rebellion, further fueled by the fall of the pro-Western monarchy in Baghdad in July of 1958. Soon the American Marines landed in Beirut from the American Sixth Fleet and did not leave until the commander of the Lebanese army, General Fouad Shehab, was elected president with the blessing of all concerned including the Maronite patriarch and President Nasser.

The Shehabist Doctrine

President Shehab's term of office was characterized by the excessive use of army officers in key posts, the rise of the notion of state security based on the expanded activity of army intelligence operatives and justified by a failed coup d'état, and the building of institutions to apply sectarian parity, fifty–fifty, in the hiring of government employees. In 1964 he was succeeded by Charles Helou, a lawyer and writer handpicked by Shehab and handled by Shehabist army officers. During Helou's term, the catastrophic defeat of Egypt and Syria in the 1967 war fueled the rise of Palestinian guerilla organizations under the umbrella of the Palestine Liberation Organization (PLO). In open defiance of Lebanese authorities, those groups based themselves in and commenced their operations from South Lebanon in what came later to be known as Fatah Land.

The Palestinian Factor

Lebanese sympathy to the Palestinian cause brought the wrath of Israel on Lebanon. On December 31, 1968, the Israeli army launched an unprovoked attack on the Beirut International Airport, landing soldiers who briefly held the airport and used explosives to destroy every Lebanese civil aircraft that happened to be there, amounting to the majority of the civil aircraft fleet of Lebanon, and signaling the beginning of a long and never-ending war between Lebanon and Israel. On November 3, 1969, the commander of the Lebanese army at the time, General Emile Boustani, signed an agreement with the PLO in Cairo. The Cairo Agreement, as it came to be known, officially permitted PLO military activities in certain areas of

South Lebanon and ceded Palestinian refugee settlements to PLO control.

The rapid expansion of Palestinian military muscle in Lebanon, with PLO chairman Yasser Arafat taking military control of a large section of Beirut for his headquarters, and the lack of an official Lebanese political will to check the Palestinian activities after their very close encounter with the Jordanian army in 1970, fueled sectarian tensions among many Lebanese and provided an excuse for the organization of armed private militias. A general breakdown of law and order followed the attack on a Palestinian bus transiting the neighborhood of Ein el Remmaneh on April 13, 1975, and the massacre of all its passengers, and precipitated a civil war between the PLO forces and their Lebanese allies under the umbrella of the National Movement (NM) led by Kamal Jumblat on the one hand and the Christian forces of the Tigers, of former president Camille Shamoun, the Phalange Party, and their allies. Some elements of the now-fragmented Lebanese army joined forces on both sides. When the Christian military front collapsed in a matter of hours, the Syrian army entered the country, with the open and active support and consent of the big powers led by the United States, and swiftly ended the fighting. Syria's occupation of Lebanon was blessed by the Maronite Christian leaders and camouflaged as an Arab League initiative. The Syrians checked but did not try to expel the PLO. They simply put it on a leash. In 1976 a new president was elected, Elias Sarkis, who was a high-ranking civil servant of the Shehabist era and a close ally of Shehab. He was elected in May, 1976, in a hotel in the Bikaa under the protection of the Syrian army.

The South Lebanon Army

The unraveling of the Lebanese army gave Israel an opportunity in the South Lebanon town of Marjioun, where an army garrison was besieged by the PLO and its allies and could not be reached or resupplied from Lebanese territory. A Lebanese army officer, Major Saad Haddad, took command of this garrison by traveling via Israeli-held territory. Subsequently he became an Israeli ally, and the Lebanese army garrison developed into the South Lebanon Army (SLA), wholly financed, equipped, and controlled by Israel. The largest of the Christian militias was borne of the Phalange Party, and after subduing by force the rival Tigers militia, it came to be known in the late 1970s as the Lebanese Forces (LF). The LF was heavily trained, armed, and financed by Israel. In 1978 the Israeli army staged a controlled invasion of South Lebanon and, in close cooperation with Major Haddad's force, established a "security belt" as a buffer to protect Israeli territory. Limited Israeli operations continued on Lebanese territory intermittently until Israel launched a major invasion on June 4, 1982, which ended the official PLO presence in Beirut and military presence in South Lebanon, with the exception of the Palestinian refugee settlements. The commander of the LF militia, Bashir Gemayel, son of the founder of the Phalange

Pierre Gemayel, was elected president during the Israeli occupation. He was assassinated following the eviction of the PLO forces from Beirut. This was followed by the massive massacre, in the poor Beirut suburb of Sabra and Shatila, of several hundred civilians, Palestinian and Lebanese, by LF militiamen in revenge for the assassination of Bashir, and the election of Bashir's older brother, Amine, as president, with full Israeli and American support. Multinational European and American forces had already landed in Lebanon, led by the American Marines and their French equivalents. They departed following several major attacks, with hundreds of fatalities, including the blowing up of the Marine compound at the Beirut Airport, the headquarters of the French paratroopers not far from there, and the American embassy.

The Iraq War and President Bashar Assad

The United States military returned to the Middle East region in force in 1990 to roll back the Iraqi occupation of Kuwait, and in 2002–2003 to invade and occupy Iraq and Afghanistan. In spite of its support for the first Gulf War under President Hafez Assad (Assad I) which was directed by President George Bush, the Syrian government under President Bashar Assad (Assad II) did not support the second Gulf War, which was launched by the second president Bush, George W. Bashar was suspected of harboring a secret agenda to support the Iraqi resistance to US occupation. Hence Syria's relationship with the United States deteriorated. As the Iraq War worsened, President Bush signed into law on December 12, 2003, the Syria Accountability and Lebanese Sovereignty Restoration Act of 2003, designed to pressure Bashar's government to work more aggressively in fighting terrorism at home and in Iraq. The new law authorized a combination of punitive economic sanctions and diplomatic measures. This signaled a new round of confrontation between the United States and Syria. The first battle in this confrontation was in Lebanon. The term of the Lebanese president Emile LaHood was to expire in November of 2004. LaHood, like many of his predecessors, was elected while Syrian troops occupied much of Lebanon. He was considered an ally of President Assad. Like most previous Lebanese presidents, LaHood wished to have a second term in office, although reelection was explicitly forbidden by Article 49 of the constitution. Parliament had the term of his predecessor, Elias Hrawi, extended for three years through a constitutional amendment. LaHood thought it was fair for him to receive a similar extension. But the United States and France, which had earlier cast a blind eye on Hrawi's term extension, were now openly opposed to the LaHood extension. After months of speculation on this issue, a semi-official press release was issued on behalf of LaHood on Tuesday, August 24, 2004, asserting his willingness to serve a new full term in office pursuant to a new constitutional amendment, against the wishes of the United States and its allies.

The Shift from Al-Sharia to French Law

For the most part of the nineteenth century and the early part of the twentieth, the Ottoman sultanate underwent vast legal reforms as part of a comprehensive modernization process to enable its full participation the European community of nations. The centerpiece of the reforms was the codification of the *fiqh* of Al-Sharia according to the *Hanafi* school. The new code was called *Majallat al Ahkam al Adlyyat*, or the Code of Justice Rules. A significant part of this code is still in force in Lebanon. In the early part of the twentieth century, two more modern Ottoman laws were enacted: the Code of Judicial Procedure, which remained in force in Lebanon until superseded by the Code of Civil Procedure in 1932; and the Law of Associations, which remains in force to the present day.

Suspension of the Islamic Rule of Law

When the French expeditionary force landed in Beirut in October, 1919, there was already a strong legal tradition in place based on a rich mix of Al-Sharia and modern Ottoman codes, giving rise to a distinctive and powerful Islamic Rule of Law, which the French proceeded to put an end to without ever succeeding in establishing an equally viable alternative.

The French generals and other high commissioners who followed pursuant to the military occupation and the League of Nations Mandate saw to it that the Republic of Lebanon did not only have a liberal constitution modeled on the French one, albeit with restricted sovereignty, but that a series of statutes were issued modeled on French law. The jurisdiction of Al-Sharia courts, which before Gourau exercised general jurisdiction as the courts of common law, was restricted to family law and inheritance, and their common law role was replaced by a new system of civil courts modeled after the French judiciary, with a backbone of mixed courts where Lebanese and French judges sat side by side in tribunals often chaired by French judges. As a result, Lebanon received a legacy of civil law that, bit by bit, superseded the Al-Sharia system. What enabled this vast legal development was the establishment in Beirut in 1913 of a Jesuit law school affiliated with a French university at Lyons. This school did not become fully functional until the French occupation of Lebanon. Most of its students were Maronite. From there on it supplied all the judges and a majority of the legislators, ministers, prime ministers, and presidents. Until the late 1950s it enjoyed a total monopoly on legal education in Lebanon. If it had the rule of law among its mission statement, it certainly did not make much of a success of it.

A New Call for the Protection of *Ahl-ul-zimmat?*

The Maronite Church, followed by the Maronite political establishment, not only sought to maintain the privileges enjoyed by the Maronite community under church leadership in the Ottoman Empire in accordance with Al-Sharia, and to expand those privileges, but also opted to ignore Article 7 of the Constitution calling for equality of the Lebanese without discrimination. This slowly but surely gave rise to a growing reaction among other groups led by communal politicians who called for similar or opposite privileges. A perverted political discourse took hold, and continues with frightening manifestations to this day, marked by conflicting calls for "restoring" and/or "safeguarding" the perceived rights of each and every group defined by religious affiliation, but not of human rights or the rights of citizens. When the number of Maronites in Lebanon dwindled dramatically, the Maronite Church, followed by Maronite politicians, openly sought reinforcement of protection for the old privileges, much in the *zimmat* tradition. In a way the Maronite Church and politicians may not have realized, they effectively voted for the restoration of the Islamic Rule of Law, with all the safeguards it embodies for minorities, and against the Civil Rule of Law based on the notion of equality and nondiscrimination among or against Lebanese citizens. Such behavior, and the behavior of the Maronite political establishment as a whole, makes the return of the Islamic Rule of Law under Al-Sharia inevitable.

Among the most elementary requirements for the Civil Rule of Law, which Lebanon had to observe as a constitutional republic, is the development of a body of statutes sanctioned by a legitimate legislature, constitutionally established (i.e., a duly elected parliament). This task has been mostly fulfilled by borrowing and Arabizing texts from French law. But so far many other necessary requirements have not been met, such as:

A. The existence of one legitimate constitutional government, recognized by the people as legitimate and sovereign, with all three branches constituted as per the constitution: the executive (Council of Ministers), the legislative (parliament), and the judicial (courts of law), equally under and governed by law and fully accountable in accordance with the law under conditions of honor and integrity.
B. Equality under the law, with no discrimination for reasons such as religion or gender, already provided under Article 7 of the Constitution.
C. Equal application of the law, which requires consistency in interpretation of the rules and in their application to citizens.
D. Respect for human rights, particularly in the prevention of arbitrary detention and all forms of torture, safeguarding the rights of defense and avoidance of denial of justice.

Lebanon's dismal failure on all these fronts flagrantly and flatly contradicts its wholesome subscription, in its statute book, to the Western European legal model.

The alternative would have been for the Maronite Church and political establishment to recognize that, in the long run, real and effective protection for the Maronites is the same as real and effective protection for all other Lebanese, and lies mainly in the recognition of the equality of all Lebanese citizens based on human rights and the equal protection of the law under the Rule of Law. This alternative is still open but may soon vanish. Choosing this alternative would necessitate a swift and convincing change in the political discourse, beginning with the dropping of the "rights of Christians" and the "rights of Muslims" slogans and the launch of a credible effort to put together a communal blind political coalition to wage a national campaign for the Civil Rule of Law.

There is little doubt that Lebanon has no future as an independent and democratic political entity without the establishment of, and full respect for, the rule of law. The question is, which rule of law? A rule of law on the legal tradition Lebanon borrowed from Western Europe, which may be referred to as the "Civil Rule of Law," or a rule of law based on Lebanon's pre-statehood and original tradition of Islamic law, which could correctly be called the "Islamic Rule of Law"? The apparent failure so far of the Civil Rule of Law will make the comeback of the Islamic Rule of Law inevitable.

Section Seven

THE RELATIONSHIP OF MUSLIMS TO NON-MUSLIMS OUT OF DAR AL-ISLAM

Chapter Twenty-Two

DAR AL-AHD AND DAR AL-HARB

The translation of the above Arabic title is "the House of Covenant" and "the House of War." Non-Muslims who are not in Dar Al-Islam may enter into two types of covenants with Muslims:

(1) A general covenant of indefinite duration which takes the form of a treaty between the Islamic state and their respective state. This covenant will cover all the subjects of each such state in the territory of the other state; and/or

(2) A special covenant valid for an agreed term for all such subjects or just for permitting Muslims to enter the territory of the other state and/or vice versa. Such a covenant could be private and issued to one person at a time.

These covenants give rise to *Dar Al-Ahd.*

All that is outside Dar Al-Islam and *Dar Al-Ahd* is *Dar Al-Harb,* the House of War, and its natives are called *harbeyeen,* plural of *harbey,* war-wagers. This does not at all mean that Dar Al-Islam is in a constant state of war with *Dar Al-Harb,* for Muslims may not carry on war except in self-defense or for the recovery of their usurped *dyar.*

> "Fight on the path of Allah all those who fight you. Do not commit aggression. Allah dislikes aggressors." (*Al-Baqarat* 190)
>
> "He dislikes aggressors." (*Al-a'raf* 55)
>
> "Whoever transgresses against you, transgress against him equally." (*Al-Baqarat* 194)
>
> "You are commanded to fight although it is something you hate." (*Al-Baqarat* 216)
>
> "They said: how can we not fight in the path of Allah after we were driven out of our homes." (*Al-Baqarat* 264)
>
> "Drive them out of where they drove you out." (*Al-Baqarat* 191)
>
> "Allah does not forbid you from being charitable and just to those

who did not fight you for your religion. Allah loves the just. But Allah forbids you to do so to those who fought you for your religion and evicted you from your homes." (*Al-Mumtahenat* 8, 9)

"If they disengaged, stopped fighting you and offered you peace, Allah forbids you from going against them." (*An-Nisa'* 90)

War on some Muslims is a war on all Muslims, but this should not be done in violation of a covenant.

A *harbey* who is apprehended in Dar Al-Islam without the benefit of a general, special, or private covenant is not killed or jailed but is safely deported to his country.

In modern terms, the recognition of a foreign state, done in reciprocity, constitutes a covenant which removes that state from *Dar Al-Harb* and places it in *Dar Al-Ahd.* An official visa by an Islamic state to a foreign individual constitutes a private covenant. Under this covenant the visa-holder submits to Al-Sharia, including recompensation. If he violates the terms of his entry, he is deported. In return he enjoys full protection of the host state just like a Muslim does.

Chapter Twenty-Three

MUSLIMS OUT OF DAR AL-ISLAM

The relationship of Muslims with non-Muslims out of Dar Al-Islam may only exist under reciprocal covenants. If it falls under a general covenant with a country of *Dar Al-Ahd*, the relationship is governed by the conditions of such a covenant. If there is no such covenant, and the Muslim is actually a citizen of such a country, then the relationship between the Muslim and his country would be subject to the covenant entered into between all the citizens of the country, which provides safeguards equally for all. Such a covenant is normally enshrined in the constitution and protected by the rule of law, so that everybody is protected by the constitution and laws and is not subject to the caprice of the rulers. If such caprice exists and takes an oppressive form, Muslims have every right to resist and/or fight back.

In the above-referenced constitutional states, Muslim citizens have the obligation to peacefully and actively seek to uphold Al-Sharia pursuant to the local constitutional processes in force.

Chapter Twenty-Four

SHOULD THERE BE ONE MUSLIM STATE IN DAR AL-ISLAM?

Under Al-Sharia, it is not important who is the ruler. What is immensely important is the upholding of *Al-Haqq* pursuant to *Hukmul-lah* in order to support *Al-Qawa-ed* of Al-Sharia and to apply the rules provided thereunder with the ultimate aim of enforcing the safeguards that benefit all Muslims equally as individuals, families, or societies. This certainly requires a state under Al-Sharia, a Muslim state, to take charge, but not necessarily one single state.

If one state on all of Dar Al-Islam is not feasible, it should be possible within *Al-Ummat* of Al-Islam to establish more than one state. But every such state should uphold Al-Sharia and protect the *hurumat* of Allah. Furthermore, every such state should ally itself with every other Muslim state, but without violating compacts with foreign nations validly and duly entered into and validly and duly remaining in full force and effect.

Section Eight

AL-ISLAM AND HUMAN RIGHTS

Chapter Twenty-Five

A BRIEF HISTORY OF HUMAN RIGHTS IN THE WEST

The subject of human rights is taught in the West and also worldwide with reference to four main historic landmarks:

(1) The Magna Carta, issued by the English King Henry in the year 1215 under the pressure of the nobility and the clergy.

(2) The American Declaration of Independence of 1776.

(3) The Declaration of the Rights of Man and the Citizen, issued by the French National Assembly in 1789 upon the French Revolution.

(4) The Universal Declaration of Human Rights, issued by the General Assembly of the United Nations in 1948.

The Universal Declaration was followed by a number of more detailed supplements which were called International Covenants in the areas of civil, political, economic, social, and cultural rights. A committee and a council were established for human rights within the UN. Many regional documents on human rights followed, such as the Cairo Declaration on Human Rights in Islam. The most recent significant human rights instrument is the European Convention for Human Rights, which established the European Court for Human Rights with its seat in Strasbourg, France.

Chapter Twenty-Six

A Discussion of the Western Approach to Human Rights and Al-Islam

Modern studies concerning the relationship of Al-Islam to human rights have been mostly characterized by attempts, largely by Western sources, to prove that Al-Islam is not compatible with human rights, and counter-attempts, largely by Muslim authors, to prove the opposite. An example from the first group is Professor J. Paul Martin, formerly a director of the Center for the Study of Human Rights at Columbia University, New York, who concludes, in an essay published in 2005, that "Islam is the largest single population segment where expert thinking and popular attitudes are least accepting of the international human rights regime." An example frim the latter group is Professor Mashood Baderin, of London University, who published a paper in the same year submitting that Al-Islam is an influential factor and a tool to improve poor conditions of human rights in countries that have an Islamic majority, recognize Al-Islam as the religion of the state, or otherwise recognize Al-Sharia.

Although many Muslim researchers contradicted Professor Martin's thesis by praising the human rights provided in the Universal Declaration and concluding that Al-Islam is in conformity with those rights, other Western authors heavily criticized those researchers to the extent of satire. A case in point is a recent book by Ann Elizabeth Meyer, a professor at the University of Pennsylvania. She regards the efforts of Muslim scholars as based on an apologetic course and unduly defensive in that they show disdain for Western culture and admiration of Islamic heritage instead of dealing with the human rights problems Muslims suffer from in this day and age. She notes that some Muslims treat human rights as part of the Western attempt to take control of the Middle East. Hence she believes that their reaction is political and falls within the field of resisting Western hegemony.

Like many other Western researchers, Professor Meyer asserts that an international law of human rights is in existence further to the Universal Declaration. Based on this assertion, she puts forth an argument that Al-Islam is in violation of the principles of the "international law of human rights"!

I do not believe that Professor Meyer or other Western researchers who think like her are right. Unfortunately, there is no such thing as "international law of human rights"! Furthermore, there is no "international law" apart from ratified and binding international conventions. Granted, there are also international customs, some of which were embodied in international conventions; the rest remain as mere customs.

Chapter Twenty-Seven

THE STATE OF HUMAN RIGHTS IN THE WEST

Not a single Western state recognizes the Universal Declaration as a binding international convention, because it is a mere declaration by the UN General Assembly, whose charter provides no power of legislation. Western powers do not agree that such declarations have any binding authority. They take the position that only the decisions of the UN Security Council are binding. They remind all that this organization was set up to include the states that fought with or declared war on Germany and other Axis powers during the Second World War. For example, tiny Lebanon had to declare war on Germany, Japan, and Italy as a precondition to be admitted to the organization!

It should be noted, to begin with, that the General Assembly does not consist of popularly elected representatives of their peoples but of political appointees of their respective governments. The same applies to the Security Council, where power is shared collectively by five permanent member states, also acting through their political appointees. Resolutions of the Security Council result from the heavy exercise of naked power, and hence fail every test of democratic legitimacy that national governments of UN member states are routinely subjected to.

Within two years from the day the Universal Declaration was issued, the Council of Europe launched the European Convention on Human Rights, which adopted a much more limited definition of protected rights and started the European Court of Human Rights, with compulsory jurisdiction over member states aimed at enforcing the convention.

The European Convention constitutes an act of discrimination in favor of its member states and their citizens. These have the favor and advantage of the safeguards (which are less than the safeguards in the Universal Declaration) provided by the convention, to the exclusion of the rest of humanity.

Going back in history to the Magna Carta, we find that the beneficiaries of this act represented a tiny fraction of the population. But its essence was to bring the king more under the law in favor of a bigger role for the nobility and the clergy. It had little of human rights to speak of. But the developments that followed over many centuries slowly diminished the tyrannical powers of royalty and gave rise to the concept of the rule of law in the United Kingdom and the United States. This concept compares to the French concept of *état de droit*. All this constitutes substantial progress in the direction of Al-Islam.

The French Declaration of the Rights of Man and the Citizen embodied the essential principles of the French Revolution, which was inspired by the Enlightenment and remains the foundation of the French constitution. It aimed at safeguarding the natural and inalienable rights of man, which are liberty, ownership of property, security, and the resistance of oppression.

The American Declaration of Independence asserted that God gave men the inalienable rights of life, liberty, and the pursuit of happiness.

The basic difficulty with the European (and American) approach to human rights is its strict territoriality and discriminatory character. This constitutes a big contradiction.

Napoleon Bonaparte, the favorite son of the French Revolution, did not carry with him a copy of the French Declaration when he invaded *Al-Mashreq* in the early part of the nineteenth century and committed horrible acts, such as ordering the massacre of civilians who took refuge from his soldiers in mosques. In or around 1830, French armies occupied Algeria and maintained a brutal occupation that lasted until 1962. What triggered the Algerian Revolution in 1954, six years after the Universal Declaration for which certain French jurists and diplomats took credit, was the monumental discrimination against native Muslim Algerians in violation of both declarations, the French and the Universal. Algeria had been annexed to metropolitan France, but Muslim Algerians were not considered to be citizens but mere subjects, *sujets.* Jewish Algerians were made citizens, as were French and European settlers. Terrible acts of genocide preceded and took place during the revolution.

The indigenous people of Palestine did not benefit from the Universal Declaration of 1948, which was being debated and adopted while most Palestinians were being expelled from their homes by force of arms and other means of ethnic cleansing, such as organized massacres. Their main demands were for the simple and basic rights safeguarded by the Universal Declaration. To date, the people of Palestine continue to be denied the benefits of the Universal Declaration.

Nor did the Muslim people of the Balkans derive any benefit of the Universal Declaration while they were being expelled from their home and exterminated.

Unfortunately, human rights do not apply to natural resources in disadvantaged countries which are being exploited for and on behalf of rich nations with the help of the rulers of those countries, who claim whatever revenues are received and placed on deposit, or used to buy assets, in the rich nations.

We thus face an international state of human and civil rights exclusive to citizens of the big, rich Western countries. In the United States of America, the safeguards that protect civil rights provided for in the constitution apply exclusively and only on

American soil. This is the reason why a detention facility was established on occupied Cuban territory in Guantanamo, and a series of secret interrogation centers were established in various places outside US territory. The most basic civil rights safeguards were fatally compromised by what is known as targeted killings, in which execution orders are issued by public servants against persons, including American citizens, presumed to be enemies of the United States. Other big powers had secretly followed a similar policy of killings.

Poor and weak countries are left to be cared for by privately run NGOs, which closely monitor the performance of these countries under the strictest interpretation of the Universal Declaration and decry alleged violations that come to their attention. The narrow scope of these activities, which are limited to specific cases and persons, is parallel to the ongoing political relationships which mostly bind the countries of the NGOs to the governments of the poor and weak countries that are under scrutiny. This relationship is mostly normal and cordial unless clouded by political interests that have nothing to do with human rights. Some suspect, not without good reason, that many of those NGOs have their own political agenda that is subordinate to the policies of their governments and thus are, to a large extent, political weapons against their enemies or perceived adversaries.

Chapter Twenty-Eight

A Comparison between Human Rights in the West and Al-Qawa-ed Al-Kulliat of Al-Sharia

The Universal Declaration does not fully agree with the French Declaration. But they agree on:

- Equality.
- Prohibition of arbitrary detention.
- Presumption of innocence.
- Sanctity of property ownership.

The French Declaration agrees with the Universal Declaration *and* the European Convention on the following rights and liberties:

- No slavery.
- Security and safety.
- Nonretroactivity of laws.
- Freedom of speech and expression.

The French Declaration remains unique among the above instruments in its safeguarding of the right to resist oppression.

The European Convention agrees with the Universal Declaration on:

- Sanctity of life.
- Prohibition of torture.
- Freedom of belief.
- Freedom of assembly.
- Marriage.
- Right of Privacy.

The European Convention is alone among all those instruments in safeguarding a fair trial with the right of defense as its backbone.

All the above rights and liberties are protected by *Al-Qawa-ed Al-Kulliat* of Al-Sharia *and much more*. Those rights and liberties are a testimony to the significant human progress in the direction of Al-Islam many centuries after the message was launched. In fact, *Al-Qawa-ed Al-Kulliat* of Al-Sharia are unique in safeguarding the following rights and liberties:

- Peace.
- Justice.
- Mercy.
- Sanctity of covenants and contracts.
- Sanctity of the home.
- Sanctity of *ad-dyar*.
- *Al-Irdd.*
- *Al-Izzat.*
- *Al-Ismat.*
- *Al-Karamat.*
- *Al-qisas.*
- Inheritance.

The French Declaration alone agrees with *Al-Qawa-ed Al-Kulliat* of Al-Sharia on the right to resist oppression. The Universal Declaration and the Declaration of Independence agree with *Al-Qawa-ed Al-Kulliat* of Al-Sharia that all the rights and liberties safeguarded are inalienable.

It should be noted in passing that Al-Quran mostly addresses people in general: *insan* and *nas*. The French and American declarations address men specifically. The French term for human rights is *droits de l'homme*, the rights of man.

Chapter Twenty-Nine

THE ISSUE OF RECOMPENSATION FOR THEFT

Al-Sharia is often harshly criticized for the severity of the recompensation it sets as a penalty for the crime of theft. The authority for such penalty is to be found in the following *Ayat*:

> "Cut off the hands of the *sareq*, man or woman, as recompensation for what they did." (*Al-ma-edat* 38)

The penalty prescribed is generally deemed to be in violation of human rights. Much of this criticism comes from countries that still practice capital punishment. Islam, however, found a solution to capital punishment through *afou*.

Is there an interpretation of the above *Ayat* other than the commonly recognized literal one?

Let us begin by defining the criminal targeted by the *Ayat*. In Arabic he is called a *sareq*. He is the one who violates in secret a safe place, a *hirz*, and takes from it what does not belong to him. A *hirz* is a securely protected location that cannot be easily accessed. The violation should take place in secret. In English terms, this act constitutes a burglary and not a simple theft. If the taking is done openly, the perpetrator is a usurper, perhaps a robber, but not a *sareq*, a burglar. There are other crimes involving the unlawful taking of others' money, such as fraud and embezzlement. But these crimes are not *sareqat* and their perpetrator is not a *sareq*.

The Prophet Muhammad said that there is no punishment in taking fruits hanging from a tree.

As for the recompensation of *qate'*, literally translated as cutting, two questions should be asked: whether cutting means amputating, and whether the verb is used figuratively and not literally, the intent of the imperative being to prevent or dissuade a *sareq* from doing it again. In the *Surat* of *Yousuf* it is said that women "cut their hands in awe when they saw how handsome he was" (31 *Yousuf*). The generally agreed interpretation is that they merely cut but did not amputate their hands. To cut is not to amputate.

The same term is used figuratively in the derivative *maqta'*. It is said that there are many such *maqta'* in Al-Quran, which means a place where a reciter makes a brief pause.

To cut someone's tongue does not mean to amputate it but to be charitable to its owner and to shut his mouth. The Prophet once said in this sense: "Cut his tongue away from me." It is said that a man came to the Prophet and said, "I am a poet!" The Prophet called his close assistant Bilal and asked him to "cut the tongue" of the poet. Bilal gave him forty Dirhams!

Al-Quran is full of *Ayaat* that speak of *qate'*, but clearly in a figurative sense and not meaning amputation.

> "If you were to turn back now, could it be in order to corrupt the land and cut off [your ties to] your kinship?" (*Muhammad* 22)

> "If Al-Quran were to move the mountains and cut Earth to pieces…" (*Ar-raad* 31)

> "When they saw the agony and their means were cut off…" (*Al-Baqarat* 166)

> "Go back to your Lord and ask him about the women who cut their hands." (*Yousuf* 50)

> "We cut off the last remnant of those dis-believers who belied our Ayaat." (*Al-a'raf* 72)

"Cutting their last remnant" means they will no longer beget children.

How about the word *yad*?

In Arabic, *yad* literally means a hand. It could also mean an arm. It may further mean donation and charity, which takes place through handing. It may also mean power and influence. It also means wealth and capability. It further means nourishment. It may mean a role.

> "Those who have hands and eyes..."
> (*Sad* 45)

That means physical and mental power.

It is possible, therefore, to interpret the *Ayat* of *sareqat* as applying strictly to whoever covertly violates a fortified or otherwise inaccessible place and removes from it something that does not belong to him, a burglar.

The recompensation for the act of *sareqat* is something that will end the career of the perpetrator by making sure he does not do it again. Such penalty would not necessarily be amputation but a prison sentence further to conviction upon a fair trial. Confinement will *cut* the convict's ability to burglarize again.

ABOUT THE AUTHOR

Dr. Muhamad Mugraby, a human rights defender and democracy advocate, is also a lawyer with an international practice based in Beirut. He is a former lecturer on civil rights, legal philosophy, and private international law at the Lebanese  University Law School. He was educated in Beirut, at the Lebanese University Law School and the American University, and in New York at Columbia University Law School, where he received several fellowships and the degrees of Doctor of Juridical Science (JSD), Master of Laws (LLM), and Master of Comparative Law (MCL).

For many decades, Dr. Mugraby has strongly called for the establishment of modern judicial systems in Lebanon and the Middle East, characterized with independence and integrity, as a necessary precondition for the rule of law, democracy, and modernity.

Dr. Mugraby has lectured extensively and contributed numerous articles on the rule of law and the constitution, human rights, and democracy, both in in Arabic and in English. His books include *Lebanon First* in Arabic, *Permanent Sovereignty over Oil Resources* in English and Arabic, *The Right Path Does Not Distress Me* in Arabic, *My Lebanon* in Arabic, and *Al-Islam* in Arabic.

Dr. Mugraby was born in Beirut. He is seventy-four years old. He is married to Dalal Macki Mugraby, professor emeritus of interior design at the Lebanese University at Beirut and a graduate of Pratt Institute, New York. Dr. and Mrs. Mugraby have two children: Ziad, an information technology expert and practitioner and an economics graduate of Cornell University, and Suha, a social sciences graduate of the American University of Beirut and a social sciences researcher.

Dr. Mugraby can be reached at muhamad.mugraby@mugraby.com.

INDEX

Abou Hanifat: 140-141.
Ad-dyar: 116, 138, 229.
Adl: 86, 117-118.
Afou: See Clemency.
Algeria: xi, xxi, 223, 224.
Ahd: xiv, 176, 177, 178, 179, 180, 206-207, 209.
Ahkam: 102- 211, 136, 140, 141, 198.
Akbar: 15, 19-21, 155.
Alaq: 37, 61-66, 65.
Allah: x, xii, xiii, xvii, xxi, 3, 4, 5, 6, 7, 8, 9, 10, 11, 12, 13, 15, 16, 17, 19, 20, 21, 22, 23, 24, 25, 26, 28, 29, 30, 31, 32, 33, 34, 35, 36, 39, 40, 41, 42, 43, 44, 45, 46, 47, 48, 49, 50, 51, 52, 53, 54, 55, 56, 57, 58, 59, 60, 61, 62, 63, 64, 65, 66, 67, 68, 69, 70, 74, 75, 76, 77, 79, 80, 81, 82, 83, 84, 85, 86, 87, 95, 96, 97, 98, 99, 101, 102, 104, 105, 106, 107, 111, 112, 113, 114, 116, 117, 118, 119, 120, 121, 122, 124, 125, 126, 127, 128, 136, 137, 139, 140, 144, 145, 146, 147, 148, 149, 150, 153, 145, 155, 160, 162, 163, 164, 165, 170, 171, 177, 178, 179, 183, 184, 206, 207, 212.
Apostate: 175.
Ayat: 29-30, 37, 126.
Azan: xii, 15, 21, 155.

Bara-at: 4, 123.
Basmalat: 26.

Chair: See Kursi.
Christianity: xii, 126, 179.
Clemency: 84, 147-150.
Compact: See Meethaq.
Contract: xiii, xiv, 113-116, 128, 129, 132, 133, 160, 161, 229.
Covenant: xiv, 16, 32, 55, 58-60, 76, 81, 113, 114, 116, 122, 154, 177, 178, 179, 180, 181, 205, 206, 207, 209, 216, 229.
Creed: 5, 7, 8, 9, 23, 25, 52, 57, 73-82, 95, 97, 115, 125, 153, 155, 161.
Cutting: See Sareqat.

Dayan: 48, 49, 77.
Deen: 48, 73, 77. See also Creed, Religion.

Egypt: x, xi, 179, 180, 187, 192, 193.

Fatiha: 26, 37, 39-60, 68.
Fiqh: xviii, 27, 102, 103, 111, 139, 140, 141, 158, 198.
Fitrat: 122, 123.
France: 188, 189, 191, 192, 197, 216, 224.

Ghifran: See Clemency.

Hajj: xxii, 8.
Halal: 123.
Hanif: 1.
Hamd: 48, 88.
Haqq: 21, 22, 23, 24, 30, 36, 40, 45, 49, 84, 86, 55-59, 104, 105, 106, 109, 111, 117, 125, 153, 155, 157, 162, 164, 166, 211.
Harb: 206-207.
Hisab: 143-146.
Hisbat: 159, 166, 167-169.
Hukm-ul-lah: xvii, 101-107, 135, 211, 158, 160.
Human rights: vii, viii, xiii, xv, 200, 201, 213-229.

Ibadat: 73-74, 140, 155.
Ibn Hanbal: 140-141.
Imam: 8, 42, 114, 128, 140, 153, 157, 158, 159-161.
Iran: xi, 141.

Jaafar: 140-141.
Judaism: xii, 126, 179.
Judge: 43, 49, 77, 85, 86, 87, 90, 103, 129, 140, 141, 158, 161-169, 199.

Kuffar: 183-184.
Kursi: 37, 67, 70.

Life (the right to): xiii, 22, 111, 112, 120, 122, 137, 223, 228.
Lebanon: xi, 180, 185, 202, 221, 236.

Magna Carta: 212, 215.
Malek: 140-141.
Mazalem: 159, 165-167, 168.
Mazhab: 140-141.
Meethaq: 58-60, 113.
Morocco: xi.
Muhammad, the Prophet: xii, xiii, xvii, xviii, xxii, 5, 6, 13, 15, 16, 17, 23, 24, 25, 26, 28, 31, 35, 45, 48, 50, 52, 53, 58, 61, 63, 64, 65, 69, 75, 79, 80, 82, 98, 99, 107, 114, 115, 116, 120, 122, 125, 127, 128, 129, 137, 139, 149, 153, 154, 160, 161, 163, 170, 175, 184, 232, 233.
Mustaqeem: 49, 51.

Napoleon: X, 106, 223.

Ottoman (sultanate): 106, 141, 187-198, 199.

Palestine: 186, 187, 188, 193, 224.

Qate': See sareqat.
Qawa-ed: xviii, 105, 109-138, 141, 158, 211, 228, 229.
Qayyoum: 51, 68-70.
Quran: xx, 7, 22, 26, 27, 28, 29, 31, 34, 39, 41, 49, 57, 62, 63, 67, 68, 83, 96, 97, 101, 102, 126, 127, 135, 139, 143, 154, 164, 169, 170, 184, 229, 233.

Rab-al-Alameen: 39, 46, 48, 59.
Raheem: 22, 25, 26, 39, 40, 41-60, 61, 84.
Rahman: 13, 22, 25, 26, 39, 40, 41-47, 48, 60, 61, 67, 83, 118, 146, 155.
Recompensation: 12, 77, 105, 136-137, 145, 146, 153, 155, 176, 178, 207, 231, 234.
Religion: xii, xiii, xxi, 48, 56, 73-77, 95, 179, 201, 218.
Resalat: 5, 27.

Safh: See clemency.
Sareqat: 231-234.
Sawa: 123-124, 125.
Shafe'i: 140-141.
Shahadat: 15, 16-19.
Sharia: 5, 6, 7, 8, 9, 11, 12, 18, 19, 20, 25, 26, 28,

31, 32, 35, 36, 37, 48, 58, 60, 64, 69, 76, 77, 80, 82, 95, 99, 101, 102, 103, 109, 110, 114, 116, 128, 1323, 133, 134, 135, 136, 138, 139, 141, 144, 145, 153, 154, 155, 157, 158, 160, 161, 165, 176, 178, 181, 198, 199, 200, 207, 210, 211, 218, 228, 229, 231.

Shurk: 7, 12, 22, 87, 175.

Straight (path): 10, 25, 29, 39, 49-60, 109, 133, 135, 153, 159.

Sunnat: xxiii, 5, 28, 53, 102, 139, 140.

Surat: 28, 41.

Syria: x, 180, 181, 192, 194, 195, 196, 197.

Takbeer: 15, 19-21.
Tawbat: See Clemency.
Testimony: 13, 15, 16-19, 21, 23, 25, 51, 79, 130, 154, 155, 163, 175, 228. See also Witness.

Trial: 161-165.
Tunisia: xi.
Turkey: xi.

Ummat: 17, 32, 57, 98, 153-156, 157, 159, 161, 176, 211.

Welayat: 159-169.
Witness: 13, 15-19, 88, 130, 163-164, 167. See also Testimony.

Yaoum: 18, 48.

Zakat: 76, 79, 119, 161, 168, 169-171, 178.
Zimmat: xiv, 79, 81, 176, 177-181, 199, 200.
Zulm: 9, 10, 64, 112, 111, 165.

www.ingramcontent.com/pod-product-compliance
Lightning Source LLC
Chambersburg PA
CBHW031310150426
43191CB00005B/164